# The First Lady of Radio

# The First Lady of Radio

*Eleanor Roosevelt's Historic Broadcasts*

*Edited by*
Stephen Drury Smith

**THE NEW PRESS**

NEW YORK
LONDON

Requests for permission to reproduce selections from this book
should be mailed to: Permissions Department, The New Press,
120 Wall Street, 31st floor, New York, NY 10005.

Published in the United States by The New Press, New York, 2014
Distributed by Perseus Distribution

ISBN 978-1-62097-042-3 (hc)
ISBN 978-1-62097-049-2 (e-book)
ISBN 978-1-62097-058-4 (e-book with audio)
CIP data available

The New Press publishes books that promote and enrich public
discussion and understanding of the issues vital to our democracy
and to a more equitable world. These books are made possible by
the enthusiasm of our readers; the support of a committed group of
donors, large and small; the collaboration of our many partners in the
independent media and the not-for-profit sector; booksellers, who often
hand-sell New Press books; librarians; and above all by our authors.

www.thenewpress.com

Composition by dix!
This book was set in Adobe Garamond

Printed in the United States of America

2   4   6   8   10   9   7   5   3   1

*For Kate*

# Contents

Acknowledgments                                                    ix

A Note on the Transcripts                                          xi

Foreword by Blanche Wiesen Cook                                    xiii

Introduction                                                       1

1. "The Girl of Today"                                             19
2. "Woman's Career vs. Woman's Home"                              26
3. "A Mother's Responsibility as a Citizen"                       29
4. "Concluding Broadcast"                                          33
5. "Negro Education"                                               36
6. "When Will a Woman Become President of the U.S.?"             42
7. "Shall a Woman Be Herself?"                                     51
8. "A Day in the White House"                                     56
9. "Peace Through Education"                                       62
10. "World Court Broadcast"                                        68

11. "Making the Wheels Go 'Round in the White House"   74
12. "Keeping House on a Budget in the White House"   80
13. "What It Means to Be the Wife of the President"   85
14. "Education of a Daughter for the Twentieth Century"   94
15. "Problems of Working Women"   101
16. "Life in a Tenement"   108
17. "Eleanor Roosevelt Interviewed on the Causes and Cures of War"   115
18. "Domestic Workers and Government Housing"   121
19. "Questions About the White House"   130
20. "Democracy"   136
21. "Political Conventions and Campaign Trips"   141
22. "Planning for War and Postwar Periods"   147
23. "Peace, Democracy, and Ideals"   152
24. "Address to the Democratic National Convention"   158
25. "Shall We Arm Merchant Ships?"   161
26. "Freedom of Speech"   172
27. "Propaganda"   177
28. "Isolationists"   182
29. "Pearl Harbor Attack"   189
30. "Civilian Defense"   198
31. "Preparedness for War"   204
32. "Enemy Aliens and Women in War Work"   210
33. "Answering Her Critics"   216
34. "Broadcast from Liverpool"   220
35. "Wartime Conditions in Great Britain"   227
36. "D-Day Message"   237
37. "V-E Day Radio Message"   239
38. "V-J Day Radio Message"   241

Notes   245

# Acknowledgments

Many people have supported the public radio documentary projec: that also gave rise to this anthology. I want to thank my colleagues at American Public Media™ and its documentary unit, American RadioWorks®. I am indebted to the staffs at several archives, including the Franklin D. Roosevelt Library, the Library of Congress, the National Archives and Records Administration, the Library of American Broadcasting at the University of Maryland, and the Special Collections department of the University of Wisconsin–Madison Libraries. For help with the manuscript, I am grateful to historians Maurine Beasley and Brian Horrigan, and intern Minna Zhou.

# A Note on the Transcripts

The transcripts for this book were primarily drawn from typewritten
radio scripts in the Eleanor Roosevelt papers collection at the Franklin D. Roosevelt Library in Hyde Park, New York. Many of the transcripts are reproduced virtually verbatim, with small changes to include
handwritten revisions or to make punctuation meant for the ear work
better for the eye. Whenever possible, the archival scripts have been
checked against recordings of the broadcasts to ensure accuracy. But recordings for many of the programs were never made or did not survive.
Scripts often got changed at the last minute and ER was also known
to extemporize on occasion. In some instances an authoritative, post-
broadcast transcript was produced by either the network or the sponsor-
ing ad agency.

A few of the transcripts have been edited to eliminate targential
material. A few words have been added in brackets to provide context.

This anthology is not intended to be a mechanical reproduction of the original scripts. Most of the scripts can be found in the Speech and Article File of ER's papers at the FDR Library.

Where possible, I have included some of the original advertising copy, announcer continuity, and musical cues in the first selection from a given commercial series. This is meant to provide a richer sense of how the radio broadcast sounded.

# Foreword

As we contemplate the global challenges and conservative backlash against all liberal policies, Eleanor Roosevelt emerges ever more clearly as the Voice of the Century. She was a steadfast progressive, an anti-racist visionary for democracy—which she defined as political and economic opportunity with equal justice for all. In her columns, articles, and broadcasts, ER was specific: to achieve democracy, America required movements for change which would insure decent housing, adequate health care, excellent education for all—across all differences and divides, women and men in equal measure.

Since the issues she addressed as First Lady with her unique and inspiring vision are once again the most urgent issues of our time, Stephen Drury Smith's splendid collection of Eleanor Roosevelt's radio transcripts are important and generative. Independent and bold, even competitive, ER was in part FDR's political partner. She sought to enhance her husband's efforts, and build support for his best visions. When they disagreed and she sought to move him further, she wrote about or broadcast alternatives. As the First Lady of Radio, ER was full of surprises. She welcomed controversy, told secrets, revealed intimacies, and was generally more blunt than reserved. She had flair and a grand sense of humor, shared astonishing details of White House life, interviewed activists and workers, spoke clearly about refugees and race.

Justice Thurgood Marshall called her "Lady Big Heart" because of her commitment to civil rights over many decades. Indeed, her first dramatic speech for universal quality education without discrimination— addressed to educators who had just condemned segregation at the National Conference on Fundamental Problems in the Education of Negroes in Washington on May 11, 1934—is included in this volume.

Delighted by the resolution, which called for a New Deal for all children and had passed unanimously, ER strode upon the stage to confirm her support: "I noticed in the papers this morning the figures given of the cost in certain states per capita for the education of a colored child and of a white child, and I could not help but think . . . how stupid we are." Since democracy depends above all on an educated citizenry, a literate, informed, and concerned people, "we should really bend our energies . . . to giving to children the opportunity to develop their gifts . . . to the best that is in them." Excellent education was, for ER, a matter of national preservation:

> To deny any part of a population the opportunities for more enjoyment in life, for higher aspirations, is a menace to the nation as a whole. There has been too much concentrating wealth, and even if it means that some of us have got to learn to be a little more unselfish . . . we must realize that it will profit us all in the long run. . . . I think the day of selfishness is over; the day of really working together has come, and we must learn to work together,

all of us, regardless of race or creed or color; we must wipe out, wherever we find it, any feeling . . . of intolerance, of belief that any one group can go ahead alone. We go ahead together or we go down together.

Community responsibility to ensure excellent education, decent affordable housing with gardens and playgrounds, and quality health care for all remained ER's abiding themes, which were intensified and internationalized during the war. They defined democracy and the need to build a world peace movement—issues she addressed in all her broadcasts. She rejected greed and bigotry, fear and pettiness, as she pursued a new understanding to build a future of domestic amity and world peace. While bombs exploded, homes were rendered rubble, international borders became meaningless, and limitations regarding women's work and responsibilities ended. As public schools close across the nation and hard-won victories for women's health rights and citizen voting rights are canceled, ER's words resound with urgency. With this amazing collection, we have the path to ER's healing vision: our survival depends on war's end. We must learn to respect, honor, even to love each other, and recognize that our human family inhabits one connected community— dedicated to liberty, justice, and human rights.

Stephen Smith's comprehensive collection of Eleanor Roosevelt's broadcasts is perfectly timed to stir activists everywhere to continue the struggle for decency and survival—and to finally achieve ER's legacy of human rights for all.

—Blanche Wiesen Cook
July 2014

Eleanor Roosevelt broadcasts a message to the American people in 1942 (courtesy of the Franklin D. Roosevelt Presidential Library and Museum).

# Introduction

Sunday at the White House began much like any other. First Lady Eleanor Roosevelt described it as a "quiet" morning, although the staff was preparing for a luncheon of thirty guests, including close friends, visiting relatives, and government officials. President Franklin D. Roosevelt would take lunch privately in his study with his most trusted adviser, Harry Hopkins. Tensions had been steadily mounting between the United States and the increasingly belligerent Japanese. The president had been up late the night before, drafting a message to the Japanese emperor. So on Sunday, FDR was enjoying a few moments of private relaxation with Hopkins, his Scotty dog, Fala, and his stamp collection. ER was "disappointed but not surprised" that her husband passed on the big luncheon crowd.[1]

It was December 7, 1941.

At 1:47 p.m., Secretary of the Navy Frank Knox telephoned the president with news that Japanese airplanes had attacked the US naval base at Pearl Harbor. The attack would kill more than 2,400 military personnel and civilians and strike a heavy blow on the US Pacific Fleet. Before long, the White House corridors filled with military officials and political aides. ER overheard the news and said good-bye to her guests. FDR was clearly occupied, so ER spent the afternoon in her sitting room. She worked on correspondence, keeping an ear cocked to the hallway traffic coming and going from the president's study. She also revised her script.

As it happened, ER was scheduled to make her regular fifteen-minute national radio appearance that evening. The first lady's program was called *Over Our Coffee Cups*, airing on 122 stations of the National Broadcasting Company (NBC) and sponsored by the Pan-American Coffee Bureau, an organization representing seven Latin American coffee-growing countries. The program was one in a series of commercially sponsored prime-time radio shows that ER hosted while she was first lady. On that Sunday afternoon, the president dictated to his secretary the "date which will live in infamy" speech he would deliver to Congress and on national radio the next day. The first lady was across the hall rewriting her upcoming broadcast.

At 6:45 p.m. on her live broadcast, in her calm, measured voice, ER explained that the president was meeting with his cabinet and members of Congress and had spent the afternoon conferring with diplomatic and military officials. She explained that Congress would have a full report on the situation the next morning. Then, as she often did, ER cast herself as the radio listeners' fellow citizen, rather than the first lady. "We, the people, are already prepared for action. For months now the knowledge that something of this kind might happen has been hanging over our heads," she said. "That is all over now and there is no more uncertainty. We know what we have to face and know that we are ready to face it." Then Mrs. Roosevelt's words grew more personal.

Speaking to the women of the country, she noted that she had a son on a Navy destroyer somewhere at sea. "For all I know he may be on his way to the Pacific," she said. Two other Roosevelt children lived in cities on the Pacific coast and could be vulnerable to Japanese attack. ER said she understood the anxiety women would suffer over loved ones in the service or living in danger zones. But she called on American women to go about their daily business, determined to press on. "We are the free and unconquerable people of the United States of America," she said. Then ER spoke briefly to America's young people. A great opportunity to serve their country lay ahead, she told them: "I have faith in you! Just as though I were standing on a rock and that rock is my faith in my fellow citizens." With that, the first lady moved on to the previously scheduled theme of the program, Army morale, and an interview with a soldier from Fort Dix.[2]

It was a remarkable broadcast at a critical moment in the nation's history. With America under attack, the public heard first not from their president but from his wife. By going on with the show, ER could ask the American people to carry on as well. And she was careful to keep her proper place in the feminine sphere by addressing the nation's women and young people. On an evening when millions of Americans were gathering by the radio for news, it was an unprecedented moment for a first lady.

Franklin and Eleanor Roosevelt had adopted radio as a communication tool when the medium was so new no one was certain what place it would find in American culture. In 1932, the year FDR was first elected president, some 65 percent of American households owned a radio. The two primary broadcasting companies, NBC and CBS, were well established. Surveys found that listeners in the 1930s spent an average of more than four hours a day listening to radio broadcasts. By 1940, radios were in 81 percent of American households.

Franklin D. Roosevelt was a consummate broadcaster, but ER was the radio professional. During her years in the White House, ER made some three hundred radio appearances, about the same number as her husband. But for dozens of those broadcasts she got paid handsome talent fees by advertisers. Her shows were sponsored by the makers of cold cream, mattresses, coffee, typewriters, building materials, and beauty soap. It was a novel and controversial career for a president's wife. ER was criticized for commercializing her White House role and for meddling in public affairs best left to her husband. But ER was also praised for making thoughtful observations on world events, for helping unify the nation during the Depression and World War II, and for bringing Americans into more intimate contact with the White House and the presidential family.

In 1932, before FDR took office, ER declared that it was "impossible for husband and wife both to have political careers."[3] She denied having any particular political influence on the future president. But in ways both subtle and direct, ER's radio programs and other media work did far more than reflect her personal views. She helped publicize FDR's New Deal. She alerted the nation to the growing threat of world war. Once the fighting started, ER helped rally the home front. She battled her husband's critics. At the same time, her radio work challenged conventional restrictions on women as broadcasters and as political professionals. "ER set a new pace, new goals, a new understanding of what was possible and acceptable for women to achieve," historian Blanche Wiesen Cook writes.[4] ER did so in a medium, radio, that historians have argued had an "incalculable impact" on American life and politics, but that scholars and intellectuals have tended to ignore.[5]

Radio was just one of the bully pulpits ER used to influence public opinion. Her column, "My Day," was syndicated in ninety newspapers at its peak. She traveled extensively around the country and the world. Although these efforts have been widely noted by historians, far less has been said about ER at the radio microphone. In fact, few contemporary listeners have ever heard these programs.

ER was a first lady of firsts. She was the first president's wife to fly in an airplane. She was the first to testify before Congress. She was the first to hold a government job, to address a national political convention. ER's independence and determination—including her hours before the radio mike—fueled scalding criticism from those who deplored her views, disliked her voice, or thought a proper first lady should confine herself to managing domestic life in the White House. Toward the end of her first year as first lady, *Time* magazine suggested that ER was using the executive mansion "less as a home than as a base of operations." It reported on her exhaustive daily schedule, her seemingly boundless energy, and "her countless crusades."[6] A writer for *Good Housekeeping* magazine said she initially thought ER's commercial work "was not only bad judgment and bad taste but bad ethics as well."[7] Though the writer came to admire ER, the impulse was clear: first ladies, however accomplished, were expected to maintain a kind of dignified obscurity.

Today, it is unthinkable that a president's spouse would host a commercially sponsored program on radio or television or an Internet website. As Cook points out, such an arrangement would be condemned as "an illegal or immoral conflict of interest" today.[8] While it was controversial in Mrs. Roosevelt's day too, she generally shrugged off the criticism. According to historian Maurine Beasley, ER was the first president's wife to openly use the media for her own professional and political purposes. "Undaunted by the technology of modern communications, she became its master," Beasley writes.[9]

ER liked being able to talk directly to Americans on such a vast, immediate scale. She also liked the money. In the 1930s, ER earned more from a single appearance on one of her radio programs than the average American worker made all year. An independent income allowed ER to support people and charities she cared about. During the Depression, she sent some of the money to struggling Americans who wrote to her for help. Much of her radio earnings went to the American Friends Service Committee to support Arthurdale, a New Deal project for displaced coal miners in West Virginia. The experiment in subsistence homesteading became a favorite of ER's. It also mattered to ER that she have her own work with her own sphere of influence. In her broadcasts, speeches, and newspaper columns, ER would challenge conventional thinking about women and work. "Isn't it a fact that women have always worked, often very hard?" ER asked an audience in 1936. "Did anyone make a fuss about it until they began to get paid for their work?" [10]

When a letter writer from Long Island complained to ER that, at $500 a minute, she was overpaid for her radio work, ER wrote back saying she agreed. "The reason they are willing to give me this money is, of course, because my husband is the president," ER wrote. She was unapologetic: "It puts money in circulation, the money is spent for a good purpose, and these people could not otherwise be helped." [11] ER's fee put her among the highest-paid radio talent in the nation. But she didn't offer to work for less.

In her twelve years as first lady, ER hosted eight commercially sponsored radio shows. While she occasionally used the White House radio studio created for FDR's Fireside Chats to make noncommercial broadcasts, all the paid programs appear to have originated in network studios. Some programs were aimed specifically at women listeners, such as *It's a Woman's World*—a series of Friday-evening programs on the Columbia Broadcasting System (CBS), sponsored by Selby Arch-Preserver Shoes. Topics included daily life at the White House and the rigors of official entertaining. In a 1937 NBC series sponsored by Pond's, ER discussed slum housing, the problems of working women, and how to properly educate a daughter for the twentieth century. The longest-running series—and perhaps the most important one in ER's White House years—was *Over Our Coffee Cups*. The twenty-eight weekly shows ran on Sunday evenings from September 1941 to April 1942. It was ER's most overtly political radio series up to that time. She attacked FDR's isolationist critics, deplored anti-Semitism, and called on Americans to defend the free-speech rights of those with whom they disagreed.

Intellectuals "smirked at what they considered trite comments" in ER's radio programs and newspaper writing, according to Maurine Beasley, but the first lady's ideas appealed to average Americans.[12] In 1944, a writer for *The American Mercury* magazine tried to explain ER's popularity to its readership of sophisticates. ER's writing connected with common people, the magazine said, because "she expresses herself in the same sort of platitudes and clichés that they might use."[13] Blanche Wiesen Cook argues that "kernels of bold political truth" can be found "buried in boring fluff," and that the importance of ER's writings should not be trivialized. Her prose may have been plain, but the context of her message is what commands attention; no first lady had come remotely close to being the kind of public, political figure that Eleanor Roosevelt insisted on being.[14]

Radio listeners responded readily to ER's broadcasts, flooding radio stations, network headquarters, and the White House with mail. In 1933 alone, ER received some 300,000 postcards and letters. Much of the mail praised her. Jessica Alexander of Staten Island wrote, "Your little 'lecturettes' are so well chosen and so beautifully delivered that at home we look forward to Friday nights with great anticipation."[15] From Ithaca, New York, Mary Resch wrote, "We feel that you possess the ability of reaching and interesting those in high places as well as those in more lowly walks of life—the plain people—of who I am one."[16] A Republican from Summit, New Jersey, said he had never voted for FDR and did not agree with his politics, but admired ER's courage and her capacity to unite Americans, "regardless of race, creed, color or political affiliations."[17]

Letter writers were also free with their criticism. A fourteen-year-old Texas girl complained, "When I read how you get $3,000 for each radio broadcast you make, I can't help but think how unjust this world is. Here I sit, straining my ears to hear the sound of your voice with a little crystal set . . . Can't you suggest a way that I can get a radio so I can hear the music and talks and news from outside my very small little world?"[18] Pleas for money, help finding a job, or the gift of a radio were common themes of mail to ER (and to FDR, too) during the Depression. Mrs. E. L. Couture of Arlee, Montana, sent a typed postcard with this warning: "If your husband doesn't muzzle you he will be impeached before the close of his first year in the White House."[19] Betty Jones of Mattoon, Illinois, chided ER for wanting "to be too much in the limelight" for a first lady.[20] J. Winter Davis of Toledo, Ohio, wrote sarcastically about what he described as ER's snake-oil show of a radio program: "Now we have a blueblood society lady, born bred and reared in the purple, in a patronizing voice, giving us all kinds of advice. What an uplift this has been. The effect has been magical." Davis was astonished and apparently chagrined when ER wrote back to him with a firm, courteous defense of her broadcasts. He quickly replied to express a newfound admiration for the first lady's radio work: "I think it is fine, almost noble to do this, knowing as you stated that you would be the object of much criticism."[21]

Most commercial radio programs in the 1930s and '40s were produced by advertising agencies on behalf of the sponsors. Ad companies paid the radio network for air time and covered all the costs of production, including fees for the hosts, guests, and performers. Over the course of her career, ER employed several radio agents to make deals with the ad companies. Some of the biggest ad firms in New York signed her on, including J. Walter Thompson and Batten, Barton, Durstine and Osborne. ER's 1932 broadcasts for Pond's beauty cream were part of that company's larger advertising campaign in which well-known society ladies endorsed the product. She never directly recommended a product or read commercial copy in any of the programs from her White House years. But it was certainly a coup for Pond's to line up the president-elect's wife for its Friday-night broadcasts. *Radio Guide* tittered that "plucked and unplucked eyebrows arched" at ER's commercial broadcasts, and the $1,500 she was paid for each one—a salary that would be higher than the president's if annualized.[22] The *Hartford Courant* observed that Mrs. Roosevelt's career would be of no public concern if being first lady were not a full-time job of its own. Furthermore, "the dignity of the president and of the country cannot but suffer when his name is used for commercial purposes."[23]

In 1940, the liberal columnist John T. Flynn suggested that the Roosevelts' children had also enjoyed unusual success in the media based on their proximity to what he called "The White House, Inc." James Roosevelt had a lucrative job in Hollywood. Elliott Roosevelt had both management and on-air jobs in radio. Daughter Anna Roosevelt Boettiger had dabbled in radio, appeared in newspaper ads, and wrote for a Hearst newspaper of which her husband was publisher. But Flynn complained that ER outpaced them all.[24]

Conservative columnist Westbrook Pegler, initially an admirer of Eleanor Roosevelt, later became a relentless critic, not just of her but also of FDR and the New Deal. He was particularly scolding of how the Roosevelts "commercialized the presidency."[25] He reminded his readers of a 1942 broadcast ER made after returning from a wartime visit to London. The program was sponsored by what, to Pegler, was a fishy-sounding group: the Council on Candy as a Food in the War Effort. The council was a public-relations scheme backed by American candy manufacturers. There was no attempt to obscure the connection between ER and the council; it printed up attractive brochures, under the council's name, with the text of ER's remarks and a picture of her before the microphone.

During her twelve years in the White House, ER appeared on the radio more frequently in an unpaid capacity than she did to earn a paycheck. She promoted civic organizations, government programs, or progressive politics in dozens of speeches that were broadcast live on local and national radio for causes ranging from polio research to civil rights for African Americans to the Girl Scouts. Over time, the American public grew accustomed to their unusually active first lady, and, increasingly, they respected her. One NBC-backed mail-in poll proclaimed ER "The Outstanding Woman of 1937." [26] The next year, a Gallup poll found that 67 percent of Americans approved of her conduct, 33 percent disapproved—higher positive numbers than FDR's. In a 1938 poll, Hearst newspaper critics named ER radio's "outstanding non-professional." She did not have a commercial program at the time. [27]

Franklin and Eleanor Roosevelt's tenure in the White House coincided both with the ascendancy of radio as a mass medium and the rise of American celebrity culture. Movie and radio stars filled popular new magazines. Crooners, vaudeville performers, comedians, and opera stars rode the radio waves. As the first couple of this emerging mass media, Eleanor and Franklin Roosevelt revolutionized how the nation related to its chief executive and family. It's arguable, in fact, that they were the first modern couple to inhabit the White House—a couple in which each had his or her own career, political activities, controversies, and constituencies. Each was uniquely skilled in conveying the sense on radio that he or she was talking one-on-one with the audience. Americans responded to this new, conversational White House in kind. They swamped the residents of the executive mansion with an unprecedented tide of mail, much of it marked "personal."

Earlier presidents had appeared on radio, but FDR is widely regarded as the first presidential candidate to truly master radio as a source of political advantage. And he set the standard for all to follow. FDR honed his radio voice as governor of New York from 1929 to 1933. To bypass the Republican-controlled legislature and the near monopoly by Republicans on state newspapers, FDR broadcast a series of informal-sounding monthly chats to the people of New York. ER said her husband came by his command of the microphone naturally. "His voice lent itself remarkably to the radio. It was a natural gift, for in his whole life he never had a lesson in diction or public speaking," she wrote.[28]

The Roosevelts took to radio as the medium itself caught fire. The first commercially licensed radio station in the United States was KDKA in Pittsburgh. In 1920, it began broadcasting from the roof of the Westinghouse Electric factory, which owned the station and built radio receivers. Virtually no one owned a radio set, but on election night that year, KDKA broadcast news of Warren G. Harding's victory in the presidential election, passing along returns phoned in from the local newspaper. Other broadcast stations soon popped up and radio became a consumer craze.

In the 1930s, radio became a vital tool of American politics and governance. Early adopters of the new technology included populist politicians Huey Long in Louisiana and Floyd B. Olson in Minnesota, as well as the incendiary radio priest Charles Coughlin and aviator Charles Lindbergh, whose widely broadcast speeches opposed American involvement in World War II. Some social commentators believed radio would unleash new democratic energies, creating a "national town meeting" on the air. A number of programs used the town meeting motif explicitly. Others, as scholar Jason Loviglio writes, feared "hypnotized audiences falling under the sway of irrational forces like fascism, communism, or even a corrupt and bankrupt capitalism."[29]

FDR's administration understood and used the power of radio to sell the New Deal and, later, to mobilize Americans to oppose the Axis powers. The radio networks were willing accomplices. Radio came under increasing federal regulatory scrutiny in the 1930s; network executives curried favor with the FDR administration by providing free airtime for dozens of government-produced public-service programs that promoted New Deal initiatives. During World War II, the networks offered up choice slots in their schedules for war-bond rallies and home-front morale shows.

The early public discussion of radio's influence on society and culture reads much like the initial promises and dangers seen in the twenty-first-century Internet revolution. Some predicted radio would be a powerful force for democratizing information and spreading knowledge to a vast population previously divided by geography or income. But the new technology also raised anxieties. Observers worried about the propriety and taste of the radio programs that would penetrate the sanctity of the home. In 1932, journalist Anne O'Hare McCormick wrote a series of reports for the *New York Times* analyzing radio as a "great unknown force."[30] She observed that radio listening was a passive, vicarious experience with a "dazing, almost anesthetic effect upon the mind." But McCormick also saw a new mass audience in the formation: "More inclusive, more rural, more domestic, whatever you think of its taste more broadly American."[31]

Radio was the first truly *mass* medium, linking great cities and remote hamlets in the same instantaneous event. Some radio critics feared that if families stayed home with the wireless it would erode civic involvement and compete with traditional social gatherings. But others believed radio would draw Americans together as never before, creating the kind of informed, ideal republic imagined by the nation's founding generation. Historian Susan Douglas notes that Americans have repeatedly expected new technologies—the telephone, the television, the Internet—to solve society's problems.

With all the breathless predictions today about how the Internet will democratize communication and flatten hierarchies among

Americans, to bring about a new republic in cyberspace, we should remember that radio . . . was going to provide culture and education to the masses, eliminate politicians' ability to incite passions in a mob, bring people closer to government proceedings, and produce a national culture that would transcend regional and local jealousies.[32]

Radio both changed and reflected America's social conventions. For example, early radio executives had mixed feelings about women in broadcasting. Surveys showed that women listeners did the majority of the family shopping, so they were an audience that local stations and national networks naturally hoped to reel in. *Collier's* magazine noted in 1932 that "practically every sizable advertising agency now has a specialized radio staff" that included women.[33] On the air, women were generally assigned to homemaking shows, soap operas, or musical performances. There were exceptions, such as national talk-show host Mary Margaret McBride or news commentator Dorothy Thompson. But radio experts claimed that listeners of both sexes preferred male voices "for material of a matter-of-fact variety—for news and weather reports, political speeches and lectures."[34] Broadcast managers—most of whom were men—believed that "women do not like to be convinced by other women in discussions of politics and similar momentous matters."[35] Radio technicians maintained that early microphones and radio transmission equipment responded poorly to higher-pitched female voices. Given these assumptions, Eleanor Roosevelt's radio role as both a public figure and a news commentator was unusual.

This anthology represents the first collection of Eleanor Roosevelt's broadcasts to be published. Unfortunately, only a fraction of Eleanor Roosevelt's radio broadcasts survive in audio recordings. In the early years of radio, live programs could be recorded onto a flat transcription disk, the grandmother of the record LP. If recordings were made—especially of ER's first commercial programs—the disks may not have survived. Archival copies of many live programs were never made. As the technology improved, transcription recordings became more routine at the radio networks. NBC created a division to record programs in 1935. CBS followed suit several years later.

Many of the scripts for Eleanor Roosevelt's radio broadcasts are archived at the Franklin D. Roosevelt Presidential Library in Hyde Park, New York. But the paper record is far from complete. When giving a public address before a crowd or group, ER frequently spoke from brief notes or completely extemporaneously. If the speech was being broadcast nationally—as many of hers were—it is often the case that no transcript was produced, or at least did not survive. ER's commercial programs were all scripted in advance. Most of these are preserved at the FDR library. Many scripts are clearly the copies that ER used on the air. Like any radio professional, she often made last-minute word changes by hand. Hers is a distinctive and sometimes hard-to-decipher scrawl.

Piecing together a complete and authoritative list of ER's radio appearances may be impossible. She was on the radio so frequently—often as a guest on local and national programs hosted by others—that no central count appears to have been made; references to her radio broadcasts keep popping up in local newspapers and other sources.

It was sometimes a challenge for ER to fit the radio broadcasts into her crowded daily schedule. She traveled the country tirelessly, both for her own purposes and to report back to FDR on real-world social conditions during depression and war. ER's radio contracts stipulated that her broadcasts might originate from the nearest radio station as well as network studios in New York or Washington. In July 1934, ER broadcast the first of her Selby Shoe programs from Chicago, after a busy day at the Chicago Century of Progress International Exposition. In June

1937, she left the receiving line at the Delaware wedding of her son, Franklin D. Roosevelt Jr., just long enough to make a broadcast for Pond's and slip back to the festivities.

Unlike her husband, Eleanor Roosevelt was not considered a radio natural, at least not at first. *Variety* panned her initial series of commercial broadcasts as "social register ballyhoo." It said ER "speaks rather banally and abstractly—and is perhaps not the best mike voice." [36] In 1935, *Radio Guide* said "her work before the microphone left much to be desired." [37] Her voice, initially, was criticized for being too high-key. So she hired a voice coach and practiced. In 1940, *Movie and Radio Guide* ranked ER number two of radio orators; FDR was number one. By 1945, ER was praised in the *New York Times* as a model speaker, with a "kindly" voice and "smooth delivery." [38]

ER churned out a lot of words: a daily newspaper column, dozens of radio scripts, thousands of letters, speeches, lectures, essays and magazine articles, and twenty-seven books. Occasionally an advertising agency or one of the organizations she was representing would offer a draft script for her to consider. ER always insisted, however, that she was the final author of all the material connected to her name. In much of her day-to-day writing, ER appeared to spend little time on close revision. She often dictated pieces to her secretary, Malvina Thompson. In many of the radio scripts, whole sections were crossed out, a common practice to shorten the program after rehearsal so it would fit the allotted time.

By contrast, FDR and his speechwriters might labor over one of his Fireside Chats through many drafts. FDR aide and speechwriter Samuel Rosenman remembered: "The preparation of some of the speeches or messages took as many as ten days, and very few took less than three." [39] FDR also conserved his use of the chats for times of crisis or political urgency. Many average citizens wrote to him asking that he appear more often on the radio, even weekly. But Roosevelt held back. While he appeared hundreds of times on radio, it was most often while at some kind of event, such as dedicating a bridge, addressing the Boy Scouts, or campaigning for office. The Fireside Chats were different. FDR spoke slowly and directly to the American people. The nation responded by supporting his policies and electing him four times.[40]

On more than a dozen occasions, Eleanor and Franklin Roosevelt appeared on the radio on the same day, often broadcasting from different cities. They rarely appeared together on the same radio programs, and these broadcasts were generally from such public events as the laying of a cornerstone for a building. It seems they never reached into American homes, as a pair, in the kind of intimate broadcast they both specialized in separately; ER never sat down with FDR by the radio fireside.

It is unclear how closely FDR or his administration paid attention to ER's radio work. Some of his aides and cabinet members worried about potential political fallout when ER addressed racial prejudice or other controversial topics. In an autobiography published after FDR's death, ER said, "He never asked me to refrain from speaking my own mind."[41] But in 1936, the *New Yorker* reported that FDR either instructed or asked ER to decline a series of thirteen commercial broadcasts. "He has put his foot down several other times, too. We don't know what the objections have been," the article said.[42] It was an election year in 1936, and ER kept a markedly low radio profile. She did no commercial broadcasting that year, and made far fewer unpaid radio appearances than in other years.

In 1939, columnist Arthur Krock discerned an increasing level of coordination between FDR's political agenda and ER's statements and writings. They were clearly a "political team," he wrote.[43] Blanche Wiesen Cook points out that while FDR rarely acknowledged ER's influence, he encouraged her to engage in the public debate on issues. Cook writes: "She served as a sounding board and a front runner. He knew he could restrain her, but he rarely tried."[44] Samuel Rosenman said ER would often read a draft of the president's speeches, and was "very helpful" on scripts related to youth, education, or consumer interests.[45] Joseph Loviglio contends that FDR's radio speeches tended to emphasize national unity, while ER's radio talks emphasized diversity and respect for social, cultural, and gender differences. Historian Doris Kearns Goodwin observes that the Roosevelts were extraordinary political allies, and that they relied on each other to achieve their separate, sometimes parallel, goals. Goodwin writes, "She was the agitator, he was the politician."[46]

FDR died on April 12, 1945, just a few months into his fourth term as president. When her coffee-sponsored program ended in 1942, ER had ceased doing commercial radio broadcasts for the duration of the war. But during wartime she appeared frequently on radio to promote the Allied effort. Less than a month after FDR's death, on May 8, 1945, ER made a brief broadcast to mark V-E Day. In the following months and years, ER would be deeply involved in building public support for the United Nations. In December 1945, US President Harry S. Truman appointed ER as a delegate to the United Nations General Assembly. She played a central role in drafting the Universal Declaration of Human Rights. Historian Allida Black observes that once ER was "freed from the constraints of the White House," she challenged American liberals to fight harder for civil rights, civil liberties, and world cooperation.[47]

Three years after the death of her husband, ER resumed her commercial broadcasting work. In 1948–49, she appeared on a daily American Broadcasting Company (ABC) radio program with her daughter, Anna Roosevelt. It was called *The Eleanor and Anna Roosevelt Show*. Anna hosted while her mother checked in from various parts of the country and the world. Topics ranged from homey subjects to international relations. In 1950, ER teamed up with her son Elliott for a daily, forty-five-minute program on NBC. The 12:30 p.m. slot became available when veteran daytime broadcaster Mary Margaret McBride switched from NBC to ABC. It was a peculiar rivalry—if it even was a contest—because ER and McBride were old friends and even appeared on each other's programs. In the course of 233 broadcasts, Eleanor and Elliott Roosevelt interviewed a wide range of notables, from the colorful actress Tallulah Bankhead to author John Steinbeck to D-Day hero Gen. Omar Bradley. Critics praised Mrs. Roosevelt's performance but lamented her son's sometimes crass readings of commercial announcements that linked ER with the product being pitched.

Like many other radio veterans, ER made early forays into television. She both hosted and appeared on current-events programs. But radio was a more familiar and natural fit. The intimacy and reach of network radio helped ER humanize and expand the conventional dimensions of the first lady's role. Many people hated her and her husband. But millions of Americans came to regard Eleanor Roosevelt as a frequent and welcome guest in their homes, sitting down next to the radio as if they were sitting next to her. In 1940, one of those listeners was Rosa Allen in Long Beach, California. Allen wrote to Eleanor Roosevelt, "No other First Lady of the Land has ever thought [to] give quite so much attention to the people at large, and I want to assure you that this has brought you very near the hearts of most of us."[48] In 1934, Marie Hurley wrote to say that, as a "shut-in at the age of 84," she was blessed to be able to hear the voice of "the most remarkable woman, who has to my knowledge, ever occupied the White House."[49]

# 1.

# "The Girl of Today"

*The Pond's Program*

Friday, December 9, 1932, 9:30–10:00 p.m. (NBC Red Network)

Eleanor Roosevelt sparked a national controversy with the first commercial radio broadcast she made as the president-elect's wife. The program was sponsored by the makers of Pond's Cold Cream. Some Americans were offended that the future first lady seemed to be cashing in on her increasing celebrity. But thousands of others were outraged at what ER had to say about girls and alcohol.

FDR had won the 1932 election in a landslide. He and the Democrats ran on a platform that called for the repeal of the Eighteenth Amendment to the Constitution, otherwise known as Prohibition. In an era when Prohibition was a hotly debated topic, Eleanor Roosevelt described herself as "personally absolutely dry," though she occasionally took a drink.[1] In the 1928 presidential contest, ER campaigned vigorously for Democratic candidate Al Smith, who ran as a "wet" anti-Prohibition candidate. In her talk on "The Girl of Today," ER described the many positive ways that society had evolved since her day, and she welcomed the wider range of opportunities open to young women. But she suggested that Prohibition created a climate where young people were more exposed to liquor than in previous generations. She regretted that "the average girl of today faces the problem of learning, very young, how much she can drink of such things as whiskey and gin and sticking to the proper quantity." Consuming alcohol was still illegal in 1932; it would be another year before Prohibition was repealed. Biographer Joseph Lash contends that ER was not urging girls to imbibe but was underscoring the failure of Prohibition to curb excessive drinking.[2]

If so, many listeners missed the point. Angry letters and telegrams poured into the Executive Mansion in Albany, New York, where ER and the governor were living. A group of fifty prominent women in Topeka, Kansas, sent a letter of shocked protest. The pastor of Trinity Baptist Church in Oklahoma City was instructed by his congregation to report their "surprise and disappointment" at ER's remarks.[3] A group of twenty-two girls, describing themselves as "average girls of today," wrote to ER and said, "We are wholly unable to understand how there can be a 'proper quantity' of 'whiskey or gin' or any other alcoholic beverage."[4]

Others wrote to ER expressing support. Henry Ware Allen wrote from Wichita to say that only the "most unsophisticated and uninformed" would disagree with ER's assessment. A man from Denver wrote that all the other fellows he had talked to admired her courage for speaking "so honestly and frankly."[5] Dr. Maude E. Bleakmey cabled from Beaver, Pennsylvania, to say, "Bravo. Keep up the good work. Truth bows to no man's shrine."[6]

The flap created headlines in newspapers across the country. But ER refrained from trying to set the record straight publicly. Instead, she responded to many of the critical letters with a copy of her speech so that people who either misheard her remarks or were responding to news stories could see for themselves. To one man she wrote that she understood she could not continue to do commercial broadcasts after FDR's inauguration, but that "until March fourth I am a private citizen and have the right to decide for myself what is wise."[7] ER explained to another listener that she knew the Pond's broadcasts would provoke criticism, but she felt compelled to go forward because the money she earned could help the unemployed through the charities she supported.

The rest of ER's thirteen-week series for Pond's stuck to what must have seemed generally safer subjects of interest to women. She spoke on raising babies, working women, the virtues of chaperones, and keeping husbands happy. The nation was in the depths of the Depression when ER made these broadcasts. More than ten thousand banks had failed since the stock market crash of 1929. Only a quarter of unemployed families got any kind of government relief. In 28 percent of the nation's households, no one had a job. In this context, the subject of women working outside the home was highly charged. The 1930 census showed that 11 million women had jobs, about 24 percent of the women in the country. Historian Susan Ware says that women, especially married women, "faced strong public hostility to their very participation in the workforce."[8]

Many radio programs of the day combined popular music with commentary by guest speakers. In addition to ER, *The Pond's Program* featured vocalists and the Leo Reisman Orchestra. It was broadcast on the NBC Red Network, which had more stations and generally carried programs with wider appeal than the smaller Blue Network. NBC Blue was often the venue for so-called sustaining programs, which the network produced without a commercial sponsor. Sustaining programs typically involved speeches, serious dramas, educational productions, and patriotic appeals.

ER used the money she made from her early commercial radio work to support two places in New York City where unemployed women could get lunch and rest. One was in the Women's Trade Union League clubhouse, the other at the Girls' Service League headquarters. ER also gave money directly to people who wrote asking her for help. "I do not question that I often gave to people who were not worthy," she later recalled, "but in those years it seemed better to take that risk than to fail those who were worthy."[9] ER eventually directed the bulk of her commercial radio earnings to the American Friends Service Committee.

ER made her final Pond's broadcast the evening before FDR's inauguration. She explained to her audience members how she pictured them in her mind's eye as she made her talks. While ER had told the press that she would cease her commercial activities once FDR took office, she hinted to listeners that she might be back if she felt she had helpful or important words to say. "I shall always hope in one way or another to keep in touch with you, the American people."[10] That, she would.

ANNOUNCER: *The Pond's Program,* presented by the makers of Pond's Cold Cream and Pond's Vanishing Cream, under the direction of Leo Reisman!

(ORCHESTRA: "LOVE ME TONIGHT" MEDLEY)

ANNOUNCER: When something nice happens once you think it might be luck. But when it happens thousands and thousands of times you know it can't be luck. That's why you can be so sure the two Pond's Face Creams will beautify and protect your complexion. These two famous creams are adding to the loveliness of thousands and thousands of women all over the world. Many women who don't have to think about cost prefer these reasonably priced creams to all others because they have found by experience that the two Pond's Creams have special beautifying qualities.

Pond's Cold Cream cleanses the skin and then lubricates it too. The pure, delicate oils go to the bottom of every pore and float the dirt to the surface and at the same time make your skin soft, flexible, alive. Pond's

Vanishing Cream gives your skin a satiny finish and provides a perfect powder base, and then in addition protects your skin against the wind, sun, and dust.

Why put off getting the lovely complexion you can just as well have? Begin tomorrow to use the two Pond's creams, Pond's Cold Cream and Pond's Vanishing Cream.

(ORCHESTRA: "DRUMS IN MY HEART")

ANNOUNCER: Ladies and gentlemen! We are proud and happy to present tonight the first of a series of informal talks by a distinguished and charming woman, Mrs. Franklin D. Roosevelt, the wife of the president-elect of the United States. Mrs. Roosevelt will speak to the Pond's audience on live, human topics of interest to every man and woman. Tonight she is going to consider some of the problems that confront the modern girl. It is an honor to present Mrs. Roosevelt!

ER: It is almost impossible to compare the girl of today with the girl of thirty or forty years ago, not because the girls have changed, in spite of what some of my contemporaries think, but because the world we live in has changed so greatly. When I was eighteen, automobiles existed but they were still rare enough to cause the horse I was driving, in the quiet country spot on the Hudson where we spent our summers, to leap over a stone wall, taking the two-wheeled cart and its occupants with him! It was all so sudden that I came to see the horse grazing in the field, while we picked ourselves up off the ground and saw a disappearing car in the dim distance! Now my children's horses take an automobile as a matter of course and even pay little attention to an airplane flying low overhead!

It isn't, however, so much the fact that we now have all these new inventions, such as cars and airplanes, telephones, radios, electric lights and movies, but the change which they have wrought in the speed of life. We can know and see so many more people, we can do so much more in a day, even if we have work to do in our homes. It is so much easier and quicker to do if you can afford to use modern inventions that the girl of parents who are moderately well off, even a girl on a farm, may do things that would have been out of the question when I was young.

My generation's problems fundamentally were much the same as are the problems of the girl of today. We had home responsibilities and we accepted them or shirked them much as does the girl of today. But our chief preoccupation was getting to know people, girls and boys, and making friends. We were having as good a time as we could have, doing some work and incidentally finding out what in this world—which at that time we felt largely was created for us alone—really was of interest to us and vital enough to become a permanent part of the life which we were planning for ourselves.

Isn't this about the same thing which the girl of today is doing? Only instead of horses and buggies, she has a roadster or sedan. Instead of going to one place in a day and seeing a few people, she can go to four or five and see an almost unlimited number. Instead of being tied down many hours by work at home or in a shop, she has more hours to play. Instead of seeing her friends at home, or in a neighbor's house, she goes to a movie in a nearby town, to people's houses whom her parents do not know, or to a dance hall away from home. There is greater opportunity to develop, perhaps, and with wise parents the girl of today is perhaps earlier able to judge between worthwhile people and undesirable ones. She is better able to take care of herself because her experience is greater.

But on the other hand, there are more temptations and they come courting her more frequently. She is away from parental supervision much younger than was the case in my youth. Unless the parents have been wise and trained her young to judge for herself, and decide between right and wrong, she is apt to have some rather bitter experiences. Also she will have some sad disillusionments about people. For youth is apt to clothe the object of its enthusiasms with the virtues which a fertile imagination can produce, and it is a sad awakening to find that human nature is far from perfect, and that people cannot always be trusted.

In my youth, all of us saw wine upon the table in our homes. And many of us saw a good bit of excessive drinking. But very few girls, whether in high school or private school or college, drank anything beyond a glass of wine at home. And it never would have occurred to the young man to carry a flask to an evening party. He carried it traveling or on a hunting trip, but not to social gatherings, for his host provided him with whatever might be necessary. And it did not brand a girl as a prig or unsocial if she did not join in whatever conviviality was going on in the way of drinking. But Prohibition seems to have changed that to a certain extent. So that the average girl of today faces the problem of learning, very young, how much she can drink of such things as whiskey and gin and sticking to the proper quantity.

One of the things that we hoped for in Prohibition was protection for the weak, and I regret to say that I feel that conditions brought about by Prohibition require more strength of character than any conditions that I remember in my youth. The greater freedom of manners makes for franker and freer associations between young men and women today. Some people think this a pity. Undoubtedly, some of the old mystery and glamour is gone. But perhaps, on the whole, it is not a bad thing that boys and girls know each other a little bit better nowadays.

In one essential, things are undoubtedly far easier for the girl of today than they were for girls of my generation. There are more avenues open to her for education and more ways in which she can earn a living and have an interesting life. For this reason I feel that, on the whole, the girl of today, if she has sympathetic and wise parents, has a better chance of facing her problems successfully and making her life a valuable and interesting one than had the girl of thirty years ago.

(ORCHESTRA: SIGNATURE THEME)

ANNOUNCER: This is the National Broadcasting Company.

# 2.

# "Woman's Career vs. Woman's Home"

*The Pond's Program*

Friday, January 20, 1933

ER: I never like to think of this subject of a woman's career and a woman's home as being a controversy. It seems to me perfectly obvious that if a woman falls in love and marries, of course her first interest and her first duty is to her home. But her duty to her home does not of necessity preclude her having another occupation. A woman, just as a man, may have a great gift for some particular thing. That does not mean that she must give up the joy of marrying and having a home and children. It simply means, when we set them in opposition to each other, that we haven't as yet grown accustomed to the fact that women's lives must be adjusted and arranged for in just the same way men's lives are. Women may have to sacrifice certain things at times. So do men.

There was a time in our development in this country when the keeping of a home took all the strength and time that a woman had. That, today, is over and there are few women who have been in this country more than a short time and whose husbands earn more than the bare necessities of life, who are not able to do something besides keeping their home. They may choose to play bridge or golf. Or they may choose to do some part-time work, or even full-time work, in some job that interests them. If so, the only people to be concerned about it are the members of the family. To be sure, sometimes children resent the fact that their mother has a job and is not at their beck and call at any hour of the day or night. This is only so, of course, when her work is not needed for the necessities of life. But granted that the father provides the necessities, sometimes the children are jealous of the fact that a mother should want any interest outside of theirs. They are justified if something really vital goes out of their lives. But if their physical needs are cared for and if their mother, on her return, has enough vitality to keep in touch with their daily lives and know what has happened to them and to give them her sympathetic interest and advice, then it is probably far better for the future lives of these children that they should have to exercise a little unselfishness, a little thought for themselves and for others, because their mother is not always on hand. They have a right to expect that if they have a problem she will listen to it. But they have no right to expect that she will give up that which she loves because they would like to have her home at five o'clock instead of six o'clock.

Do not make the mistake of thinking when you are married you need make no further effort about your family relations. The very best thing that comes to a woman with a job is the fact that she has to use her brains to work her job in with her home duties. This keeps her brain from stagnating. She has something new to talk to her husband about and he never will get the feeling that she is just like the old chair which he has always sat in—comfortable, but thoroughly familiar and never changing. The job of being a home-keeper, a wife, and a mother—plus some other job or some other work—is quite a job. If any woman has the health and vitality and the desire to do both, it seems to me that it ought make for a happier relationship at home instead of a discontented one.

In this emergency, however, I am getting innumerable appeals asking that married women be not allowed to hold jobs which might be filled by married men or single men and women. That point of view is possible during an emergency and it may be necessary to voluntarily relinquish your work if the other partner is earning enough for the family to live on. But as a permanent concession to the needs of society, I rebel. For it seems to me that we have built up our nation on the theory that work was honorable, that those who could do something creative and productive might be doing some intangible good to their own souls, which if they were not allowed to express themselves in work, might mean a loss to themselves in enrichment of personality, and in their happiness, and a loss to the community at large.

The problem is always an individual one which every woman must decide for herself. But if a woman wants to work and keep her home, let me beg you, Mr. Man, to help her and not hold her back. If you are sympathetic and understanding you will find her in the end a better helpmate. And your cooperation will mean a better and happier understanding between you. If you fight she may be resentful, though she may give in to you. And you may wake up someday to find that you have a wife in your home who is an automaton—no longer a fulfilled and happy personality.

# 3.

# "A Mother's Responsibility as a Citizen"

## *The Pond's Program*

### Friday, February 3, 1933

ER: Mothers are usually so busy taking care of their homes and their children, and thinking about the children's education and their clothes, and how they can manage the family budget, and give all the members of the family what they need with the least possible expense, that it sometimes slips their minds that they have one more duty and responsibility which they cannot escape, namely their responsibility as citizens. This is a very vital responsibility because on the way that they fulfill their obligations toward their government will depend the attitude of their children towards the government and their own citizenship.

Example is always the greatest teacher, and if the child has grown up in a home where Mother and Father feel a responsibility for the community, that child will undoubtedly begin early to feel that he has a responsibility for the community. The mother can do a great deal toward bringing this about.

I remember going on a picnic with some young friends of mine one day last summer in one of the public parks of the state. And I was tremendously struck to find those girls and boys, at the end of our meal, picking up their papers and all the debris and putting it into the cans which were provided for it in every state camping ground, but which are placidly ignored by most people. I watched all this with care and then inquired if the youngsters belonged to a Boy or Girl Scout troop. I was told, no, that there were no troops near their home. So I asked them who had taught them to be so considerate of other people and such good campers, and they promptly responded, "Mother."

"She says that if the state provides us with parks, it's up to us as good citizens to see that they are kept nicely for everybody who wants to use them." It was a good example of a mother who was taking her responsibility as a citizen, and as a trainer of citizens, seriously. And making a very good job of it.

If the mother and father vote on Election Day—even though they have to give up some time and perhaps some money in order to do so—the children will be apt to ask what it means to vote and why it is important. And there is the first opportunity for our first lesson in democracy. Here is the chance to explain that, while in this country there may be many inequalities, this is one thing in which we are all equal. We all have but one vote, and we may all use that voting franchise to express our own opinions.

It is the mother's responsibility to see that questions which affect the public good in the community and in the state and in the country are discussed at the table and around the fire so that her children will really become interested in talking about something more than the small gossip about their friends and their own plans and immediate concerns.

Conversation and interchange of views is one of our great educations in general knowledge. And the mother can make out of the home a forum where real public opinion is formed. No matter how busy she is, she can probably take some part in community life. And it seems to me that every citizen should do something to bring himself in touch with the rest of the world, and have an interest in and work for the common cause.

At first the mother, because of her children, may be interested in the school board and the affairs of the school. She should be certainly interested in the sanitation and in the way in which the rules and regulations and laws are enforced in her community. [There is] a good example at the present moment right here in New York City of what individual mothers can do for the good of the children in general. Some 100,000 children are hungry and are lacking the best food. A plan has been evolved whereby every individual will find slipped around the milk bottle delivered to the door a little pledge slip asking those who are able to contribute the price of a quart of milk a day for as long a period as possible, to keep someone else's child in good health. Here is a concrete example of where a mother, if her budget will permit, can give tangible proof to her child that she is a good citizen of her community and has the good of all children at heart.

A determined group of women can sometimes effect great reforms in their surroundings. I remember a small village on a little island off the coast of Maine where the women once decided that a speakeasy, about half a mile away along the shore, was making their lives unbearable. In a body they marched down one night and burned that speakeasy to the ground and drove the man who owned it off the island. He never returned. And, as far as I could see, there was no great resentment amongst the men, who continued to lead their lives quite happily without him.

As citizens, if mothers would just get together and agree on what they wanted, I think they would find that their influence and power was very much greater than they had ever dreamed. A mother has a twofold responsibility: that of using her own influence as much as her duties will permit to bring about the end which she desires, and the power of her example on the future citizens.

These are great responsibilities, but [also] a great satisfaction because with them she can make her home and her country a safer and pleasanter place for her children. And from her interest in her own children, she will gradually realize that the well-being of all the children in the community must be of interest to her, for undoubtedly it affects her own home and her own children.

# 4.

# "Concluding Broadcast"

*The Pond's Program*

Friday, March 3, 1933

ER: I am grateful for this last opportunity to speak to the many people who have been interested enough to listen to me during these past weeks. As I have talked to you I have tried to realize that way up in the high mountain farms of Tennessee, on lonely ranches on the Texas plains, in thousands and thousands of homes, there are women listening to what I say. Listening and weighing my words against their own experiences. It seems impossible, incredible that this is true. And yet I know it is true because from many of these same isolated homes will come in a few days letters, sometimes telling me I have helped them, sometimes disagreeing with my view of life.

We have covered many subjects, most of them homely subjects, subjects which touch the daily lives of most of us. They may seem un-important, but if they are things with which we come in contact day by day it probably does no harm to exchange opinions about them. I always find that the point of view of other people adds something to my own.

I wish to thank those of you who have written me many pleasant letters and for the encouragement which comes to all of us from the knowledge that we have been, even in minor things, helpful to others. Those who have been critical and objected to anything which I have said, I also wish to thank, because they have taught me some valuable lessons. Criticism is good for us all if it does not have the effect of discouraging us.

Criticism of the young is often of doubtful value. They haven't yet reached the point where they can recognize their own mistakes or deficiencies and use criticism to good advantage. But for those of us who have lived a little longer, it should serve to clarify our ideas, make us surer of our own judgment and on the whole be helpful to us.

I want to assure you all that I have enjoyed my contacts with you and that I shall always hope, in one way or another, to keep in touch with you, the American people. For I feel you are very close to me. Your interests are my interests and I hope that in many ways we see eye to eye as to many of the questions that come up in our daily lives. The one great danger for a man in public life, or for the woman who is that man's wife, is that they may be set apart from the stream of life affecting the rest of the country. It is easy in Washington to think that Washington is the country and forget that it is a very small place and only becomes important as the people who live there truly represent the other parts of the country. I hope that my friends will feel as much my friends as they have always felt and as free to talk to me and to tell me what they think as ever. And I want to know the whole country, not a little part of it.

I shall hope, at times, to talk again to my radio acquaintances, if it appears that there is any way in which I can be helpful to them or if a subject appeals to me as of interest nationally.

In closing I would like also to thank the Pond's Company, which has made it possible for me financially to help so many things in which I am interested, and in addition has given me an opportunity to make a great many acquaintances throughout the United States.

The most important thing to me always are the human contacts which we make as we journey through life. People are different, and different things seem important to them. But to me the most important thing in the world is other people's lives. My friends and my family and my contacts with other human beings mean far more to me than anything else in life. So this is really au revoir and not good-bye. For in one way or another we are going to keep in close touch during these coming years.

# 5.

# "Negro Education"

Speech to the National Conference on the Education of Negroes,
Washington, DC

Friday, May 11, 1934, 11:30 a.m. (NBC Blue Network)

Civil rights for African Americans became one of ER's life missions. To
campaign for change, she used her role as public figure and, especially,
as an influential voice within FDR's administration. She believed that
equal treatment and equal opportunity for all citizens were essential to a
healthy democracy. ER's support for civil rights earned her the contempt
of many white Americans and, beginning in the 1940s, the surveillance
of her activities by J. Edgar Hoover's FBI. In 1939, ER resigned from the
Daughters of the American Revolution when that organization refused
to allow black opera singer Marian Anderson to perform at Constitution Hall in Washington, DC. With ER's backing and FDR's assent,
Anderson gave a concert on Easter Sunday to a racially diverse crowd at
the Lincoln Memorial.

In January 1934, ER convened a meeting of black leaders at the White House to discuss New Deal programs and how to extend more benefits to black communities. President Roosevelt dropped in to greet the visitors. It marked the first time a group of black leaders had been invited to the White House to discuss racial problems so deeply. ER promised them she would support their cause.

Civil rights was a politically perilous issue for the administration. Southern lawmakers controlled some of the most powerful committees in Congress. They could block or eviscerate the New Deal programs FDR thought essential to national economic recovery. Jim Crow laws in the South maintained a rigid doctrine of racial segregation. Racist attitudes and traditions perpetuated racial barriers in much of the rest of the country. Meanwhile, blacks continued to be lynched in the South, where the murders were either ignored by law enforcement or the white killers often went free. In 1934, ER joined a movement, which bridged racial lines, to pass a federal antilynching law. She worked closely with NAACP president Walter White to gain support for the legislation. She also pressed FDR to back the bill. He declined to speak publicly in favor of the proposed law.

Still, African Americans found the Roosevelt White House more welcoming than any administration in history. The forty-five-member Federal Council on Negro Affairs, a group of prominent African Americans, became known as FDR's Black Cabinet. Eleanor Roosevelt became especially close with black educator Mary McLeod Bethune, a member of the Black Cabinet and a New Deal administrator.

Historian Allida Black says that "there was no more ardent champion of the civil rights agenda," nor anyone at the White House who had a closer working relationship with civil rights leaders during the 1930s and '40s than Eleanor Roosevelt.[1] Still, ER held common stereotypes about African Americans as innately artistic and musical. This

1934 address to a convention of educators and officials in Washington was ER's first "forceful" speech against discrimination.[2] It was broadcast on national radio.

ER: It is a great pleasure for me to be with you this morning because I am following with interest all that you are doing in this conference. I noticed in the papers this morning the figures given of the cost in certain states per capita for the education of a colored child and of a white child, and I could not help but think as I read that item how stupid we are in some ways, for of course in any democracy the one important thing is to see, as far as possible, that every child receives at least the best education that that child is able to assimilate.

Now, that does not mean that education should not vary in different communities, because we all know that the needs of some communities are different from the needs of others, just as we know that some individuals (and this is not confined to any race) need a different type of education from others, and we should really bend our energies now, with our better knowledge of education, to giving to children the opportunity to develop their gifts, whatever they may be, to the best that is in them. We cannot all become geniuses, we cannot all reach the same level, but we can at least have the opportunity to do the best we can with what the Lord has given us.

I feel that while we have been fortunate in this country in having many fine men and women interested in the education of the Negro race, we have also been slow—many of us who are of the white race—in realizing how important not only to your race it is, but how important to our race that you should have the best educational advantages. The menace today to a democracy is unthinking action, action which comes from people who are illiterate, who are unable to understand what is happening in the world at large, what is happening in their own country, and who therefore act without really having any knowledge of the meaning of their actions, and that is the thing that we, whatever our race is, should be guarding against today.

There are many people in this country, many white people, who have not had the opportunity for education that they should have, and there are also many Negro people who have not had the opportunity that they should have. Both these conditions should be remedied and the same opportunities should be accorded to every child regardless of race or creed.

Of course I feel this should be done because of our intelligent interest in children, but if we have to put it on a self-interest basis, then it should be done for the preservation of the best that is in the ideals of this country, because you can have no part of your population beaten down and expect the rest of the country not to feel the effects from the big groups that are underprivileged. That is so of our groups of white people and it is so of our underprivileged groups of Negro people. It lowers the standard of living. Wherever the standard of education is low, the standard of living is low, and it is for our own preservation in order that our whole country may live up to the ideals and to the intentions which brought our forefathers to this country, that we are interested today in seeing that education is really universal throughout the country.

Now, I know what the facts are today, and I know that you know them. I know that in many communities people have been so badly off that they have not been able to keep up schools and pay teachers and do the things that should be done for the children of this generation. I think the federal government is trying to help in every way that it can in the crisis; but I think we have to go further back than the present crisis and realize that, even before we had the Depression, there were people in this country who did not understand that not giving equal opportunity to all children for education was really a menace. It was felt that possibly it was better not to educate people to want more than they were at that time getting, and the thought which goes a little beyond this was dormant in a great many places. This thought which had not yet been accepted will make us realize that to deny to any part of a population the opportunities for more enjoyment in life, for higher aspirations, is a menace to the nation as a whole. There has been too much concentrating wealth, and even if it means that some of us have got to learn to be a little more unselfish about sharing what we have than we have been in the past, we must realize that it will profit us all in the long run. We have got to think it through and realize that in the end all of us, the country over, will gain if we have a uniformly educated people; that is to say, if everywhere every child has the opportunity to gain as much knowledge as his ability will allow him to gain. We know that there are in every race certain gifts, and therefore the people of the different races will naturally want to develop those gifts. If they are denied the opportunity to do so they will always feel a frustration in their lives and a certain resentment against the people who have denied them this opportunity for self-expression.

I believe that the Negro race has tremendous gifts to bring to this country in the way of artistic development. I think things come by nature to many of them that we have to acquire, such as an appreciation of art and of music and of rhythm, which we really have to gain very often through education. I think that those things should be utilized for the good of the whole nation, that you should be allowed and helped to make your greatest contribution along the lines that you want and that give you joy. And therefore I am very happy to see this conference, and I have the hope that out of it will come a realization not only to you who are here but to all the people throughout the country who may be listening in today and who may later come in contact with those of you who are here, that we as a democracy in these times must be able to grasp our problems, must have sufficient general education to know not only what our difficulties are but what the government is trying to do to help us meet those difficulties. Without that ability in our people and without the willingness to sacrifice on the part of the people as a whole, in order that the younger generation may develop this ability, I think we have harder times ahead of us than we have had in the past. I think the day of selfishness is over; the day of really working together has come, and we must learn to work together, all of us, regardless of race or creed or color; we must wipe out, wherever we find it, any feeling that grows up of intolerance, of belief that any one group can go ahead alone. We go ahead together or we go down together, and so may you profit now and for the future by all that you do in this conference.

# 6.

## "When Will a Woman Become President of the U.S.?"

*The Simmons Program*

Tuesday, September 4, 1934, 9:30–10:00 p.m.
(NBC Blue Network)

A little more than a year after telling reporters she would give up commercial broadcasting, Eleanor Roosevelt was back at the microphone and getting paid top dollar for her work. On May 12, 1934, she spoke for six minutes as a guest of fast-talking news commentator Floyd Gibbons. ER spoke to farm wives on an NBC program sponsored by the construction materials company Johns Manville. She was paid $3,000. ER explained to reporters that she took the job to help sustain the work of the American Friends Service Committee. One radio writer quipped that her exceptionally high fee might lure other big names to the microphone: "One-time guest appearances may bob up with such paid guest stars as Benito Mussolini, Adolf Hitler, and Ramsay MacDonald. Mrs. Roosevelt has broken the barrier." [1] ER told reporters she would seek similar radio opportunities, but that no reference to any products would be made in future broadcasts.

That plan changed a month later. ER announced she would start a series of five radio programs as a news commentator sponsored by the Simmons mattress company. The prime-time series on Tuesday nights mixed ER's take on the news with musical numbers and commercials for "millionaire sleep" on Beautyrest mattresses. At the time, virtually all the prominent radio news commentators were men.

ER held forth on the value of relaxation, change in public schools, and a typical day in the White House. She took up the question of whether professional women could really be themselves in the workplace and whether a woman would ever be president. Along the way, ER made a number of subtle, positive references to New Deal initiatives such as relief for the unemployed and a new federal insurance program guaranteeing bank deposits. She also commented on the recent arrest of a suspect in the kidnapping of Charles and Anne Morrow Lindbergh's baby son.

The first lady also let listeners in on the relentless work schedules that she and FDR maintained. She described their days as packed with meetings and obligations that ran well past the dinner hour. She said it was rare that either one of them left their desk before midnight, presenting listeners with a view of a modern, professional couple equally engaged in public service.

In announcing the Simmons series, ER told reporters her $3,000 fee for each program would be donated directly to the Quakers. In time, her critics would challenge that arrangement.

(MUSICAL THEME: "NOCTURNE")

ANNOUNCER: The Simmons Company, makers of the Beautyrest Mattress, has the honor and privilege of bringing to you this evening your friend and neighbor, Mrs. Franklin D. Roosevelt. In keeping with Mrs. Roosevelt's active part in encouraging the development of American music, the Beautyrest Orchestra, under the direction of Willard Robison, will play "Arkansas Traveler," one of our native melodies. But first let me ask: How would you like to live like a millionaire for one-third of your life? Amazing as it may sound, you can! For you spend eight hours out of every twenty-four—a full third of your life—in bed. During this vitally important third of your life, the Simmons Beautyrest Mattress will give you the most luxurious sleep in the world—the same restful, refreshing slumber that has made the Beautyrest preferred by millionaires, as well as millions of others, all over America.

(ORCHESTRA STARTS)

ANNOUNCER: (OVER MUSIC) Patriarch of the hills. Wanderer through the Ozarks. Sing us the saga of rural life—on your ancient fiddle—happy toilers . . . free to live the night in gay revelry . . . await the start of the barn dance and the happy tunes of the Arkansas Traveler.

(ORCHESTRA: "ARKANSAS TRAVELER")

ANNOUNCER: And now, Mrs. Franklin D. Roosevelt, who is going to tell what she considers are the highlights of the week's news! Mrs. Roosevelt.

(APPLAUSE)

ER: Ladies and gentlemen, we begin with a heroic tale! A swim of five miles is an achievement for anyone! But I heard this morning that a fifteen-year-old, Lewis Deane of New York, swam five miles towing behind him a sailboat with his girl in it. The boat was becalmed just as evening came on. So young Deane slipped over the side. Holding the tow rope grimly in his teeth, he fought his way—literally inch by inch—to the shore five miles distant. Here indeed is an example of courage and determination which all of us should keep in mind when we become becalmed in our own lives.

The textile strike has dominated the front pages of the newspapers during the past few days. The public earnestly hopes that an early settlement can be effected between the employees and employers. The sooner an agreement can be reached, the better for both sides, as well as for the public. The present difficulties in industry require good leadership for both sides and a desire to cooperate in reaching a fair settlement to all concerned. The public earnestly hopes for a speedy settlement.

I notice a little item about a gentleman from New York State who thought he had lost his entire life savings—$6,100—because he was afraid to put them in a bank and forgot that he had hidden them in his mattress. The gentleman should be told that at present there is no further need of worrying when he puts his money in a bank. The deposit is guaranteed by the government up to the limit allowed on deposits.

To the youth of today who are interested in airplanes, it will probably be a matter of interest to know that the federal government during the last few days has asked scientists of seventy-one universities to aid them in finding what are known as "ghosts of the air." This means a deviation in the radio beam which guides aviators and which has, on several occasions, led them astray—a phenomenon not yet satisfactorily understood.

Now the word comes to us that the women scientists are not finding it any too easy to get jobs. Some employers say they would rather have a second-rate man than a first-rate woman. Take the case of the chemists. A chemist must carry his experiments from the laboratory through to the point of factory production. And many industries do not care to have women around in factories. Women chemists are unpopular. There is one bright spot, however, for women chemists. Men do not like the routine of making analyses, so this opens up a chance for women. Nor do they apparently like library research work. Here is another opening and for those women who have a knowledge of French or German there seems to be a chance at some of the more highly paid positions.

At the convention of dancing masters in New York this past week, it was predicted that there would be a return to more dignity in dancing and that waltzes and two-steps are to be revived. It will indeed be pleasant to revert to the dances of our youth and if you want really to be demonstrative, a waltz can most perfectly serve the purpose.

Job insurance or unemployment insurance seems to be a certainty before very long, but the exact kind of insurance we shall have is still open to discussion—is it to be contributed to by employer, employee, and the state? Or just by employer and employee? And how long a period shall it cover? Many observers coming back from Europe, where unemployment insurance has been in operation for some time, feel that while it is a good measure to meet temporary ups and downs, it would not be adequate to meet major depressions in any case. It is, however, a step which everyone will back and it seems to me that the exact form in which it passes is not so very important. But I do hope it will cover as long a period of unemployment as possible.

The touch of autumn weather we have had tempts me to think primarily of what we can do in the out-of-doors. And I imagine many people's interest will turn to the National Tennis Championship being played this week at Forest Hills, New York. The important question, of course, is whether or not America's best can turn back the threat of Fred Perry of Great Britain. And I am warned that we should most certainly look out for that attractive and colorful star from Czechoslovakia, Roderich Menzel, as well as many other of the foreign aces.

And now we have a new author-aviator in Mrs. Anne Morrow Lindbergh, who recently published a magazine article entitled "Flying Around the North Atlantic." Colonel Lindbergh could not ask for a more delightful interpreter. There is quiet humor and friendliness about this article, which everyone will surely enjoy.

People who thought they were going to make fortunes out of the sale of liquor are beginning to discover that this is not a gold mine any more than any other industry. The rush for permits in this business is slowing down. Bootleggers who wish to reform are not being ruled out, though if they have a police record they may not find it easy to enter into this business in a legal way. This brings us to the question of crime, for the bootlegger is closely allied to the whole crime situation. It is interesting to find that Mr. [Joseph] Keenan, Assistant Attorney General of the United States, in an address in Milwaukee to the American Bar Association convention, points out that public opinion will have to change before we make a really successful fight against crime in this country. In England, people give the police, in fighting and suppressing crime, far greater support than we do, Mr. Keenan asserts. I, personally, think that public opinion must demand from our newspapers and movies an attitude which will not make the [John] Dillingers of the country heroes to our small boys. Then and then only will the government's anticrime campaign succeed.

Do you ever eat hot dogs when you are motoring? Well, I understand we are to have a variety straight from Paris. It is a kind of baby hot dog called "saucisses de Francfort" and before long I expect to see signs all along the roads advertising hot puppies imported from France, Germany, and England. Strange that even in a taste like this we are not completely isolated from the rest of the world.

Out in Chicago a few days ago Lillian D. Rook, secretary of the National Association of Women Lawyers, made the statement that she expects to see a woman president of the United States. This was done at the convention of the association. We will deal a little more at length with this subject later on this evening. Much that was said in this convention was on the subject of increasing the number of women judges. This will be received with sympathy by a great many women who have a feeling that some of our laws will be interpreted more sympathetically by women judges. Now, as I promised, I will be back in a few moments to tell you what I think about a woman's chances of becoming president of the United States!

(APPLAUSE)

(ORCHESTRA)

ANNOUNCER: A breathless waiting, a touch of cool breeze unexpected and soothing and a bright full color of casual flowers—the music of a summer far away sings through the night suggesting a memory. Nay, more than a memory. All too lovely to be forgotten yet too delicate to last.

(ORCHESTRA: "LAMENT FOR THE LIVING")

(MIDDLE COMMERCIAL)

ANNOUNCER: Mrs. Roosevelt promised us that she would give her opinion of the question "When will a woman become president of the United States?" Mrs. Roosevelt!

ER: I do not think that it would be impossible to find a woman who could be president, but I hope that it doesn't happen in the near future. There are exceptional women just as there are exceptional men, and it takes an exceptional man to be a successful and useful president. Though women are doing more and more, and are proving every year that they are capable of assuming responsibilities which were considered to be out of their province in the past, I do not think that we have yet reached the point where the majority of our people would feel satisfied to follow the leadership and trust the judgment of a woman as president. And no woman could, therefore, succeed as president any more than could any man who did not have the trust and confidence of the majority of the nation, for this is a democracy and governed by majority rule.

People say no woman could stand the physical strain, but that I think is nonsense and answered over and over again by women through the length and breadth of the land. No man works harder in the fields than the farmer's wife, in her home and on the farm. Women have carried the same jobs in factories, even in mines, up to a few years ago. And besides their industrial jobs [women] have almost always carried on the work of the home. Sometimes badly, to be sure, but still that work has always been before them when the other work was done. The stories of women who clean office buildings all night and go home and get their children off to school and somehow manage to snatch some sleep during the day, and then go back to work at night and yet keep the home going would seem to indicate that while women may not have as much muscular strength as men, they have as much endurance and ability to bear strain as the male of the species.

Women have not as yet had, however, as many years of background in public life. Or as many years of experience in learning how to give and take in the world of affairs. And I personally would be sorry to see any woman take any position of responsibility which she was not well equipped to undertake and where she could not command the following which she would need for success. Someday a woman may be president, but I hope it will not be while we still speak of "a woman's vote." I hope it will only become a reality when she is elected as an individual because of her capacity and [because of] the trust which the majority of the people have in her integrity and ability as a person.

It is not a new thing for women to wield political power. They have done it through the men in the past and women have been independent rulers in their own right. Witness Catherine of Russia and Queen Elizabeth of England. In fact, birth seems to have created more confidence in some countries of the past than does ability today! The future lies before us, however, and women have a big contribution to make. So let us hope that when a woman does assume any important office, it will be because the services she can render are apparent to all.

(APPLAUSE)

ANNOUNCER: Few of us can afford the mansions, yachts, jewels or other expensive possessions of the millionaire. But all of us can afford the same luxury enjoyed by the richest man in the world when he sleeps. For the Beautyrest Mattress—the most comfortable money can buy—costs only two and one-fourth cents a day, just about what you pay for your daily newspaper! Right now your leading furniture and department stores are making a very special feature of the Beautyrest Mattress, Simmons beds, and scientific springs. See them—tomorrow— and open your bedroom door to millionaire sleep! You are invited to tune in next Tuesday night on another broadcast by Mrs. Franklin D. Roosevelt. Until then, the Simmons Company bids you good night.

(MUSICAL THEME: "NOCTURNE")

ANNOUNCER: This is the National Broadcasting Company.

# 7.

# "Shall a Woman Be Herself?"

*The Simmons Program*

Tuesday, September 18, 1934

ER: How disappointing it is that it seems impossible ever to start anything really new! Here we have been thinking that we had a brand-new deal with a Brain Trust all its own as a new discovery. And now comes the Commissioner of Education of Puerto Rico, Jose M. Pardine, to spoil all our pleasure by his assertion that the world's first New Dealer was Confucius, the Chinese sage who formed the first Brain Trust 2,500 years ago. Confucius advised China's rulers on new policies and trained special groups of young men to supply "Brain Trust" substitutes when he, himself, was busy with other matters. Alas, alack for what we thought was original!

From Nome, Alaska, comes the sad news that much of the city has been destroyed by fire. Only two business buildings, one hotel, a few residences in the northern section of the town, and the United States Radio Station were standing last night. Supplies of food are low and help is being rushed to Nome at once. The residents who were homeless must have spent the night in the open with a temperature which was as low as thirty-eight degrees and which may reach freezing at any time. Getting to Alaska by water will soon be impossible, so this is a serious situation.

To those who love horses, the fate of Dark Secret, who won the Futurity at Belmont Park on Saturday, was most distressing. After winning a gallant race and sticking until the finish in spite of a broken leg, this beautiful animal had to be destroyed. The joy of the day was completely changed to sorrow for those who witnessed the race.

From Geneva, Switzerland, we learn that Russia has been voted in as a member of the League of Nations by a ballot of thirty-eight to three. There was a certain amount of opposition led by Mr. [Giuseppe] Motta of Switzerland. The countries voting against admittance, after denouncing the Soviet political system, were Portugal, Holland, and Switzerland. Those who concurred in these opinions but simply abstained from voting were Argentina, Cuba, Luxembourg, Belgium, Panama, Peru, and Venezuela. Those most strongly urging the admission of Russia claimed that her exclusion made war more probable and that it was therefore wise to include her as a member of the League.

From the same place comes the account of a most interesting report. *The League of Nations Statistical Year Book on Trade in Ammunitions and Armaments* lists the total of the legal traffic in arms during 1932 as 32,934,000 gold dollars. The League uses only official government reports, and these it points out list explosives as chemicals, and by other subterfuges prevents a really accurate estimate of foreign traffic, which would make it possible for us to know what actually is the truth as regards the traffic in arms between nations.

From Kansas City we have encouraging news that rain has revived the West and business reports have taken a spurt. It appears that this rain will help enormously in providing fall forage for the cattle. It is wonderful what a little green will do to revive our spirits. Having seen the drought areas, I realize what it must mean. Therefore, I am grateful that Nature is helping to restore man's confidence.

A very interesting court has just been opened in New York City, which is known as the Poor Man's Court. It is in the Small Claims Division of the Municipal Court and was established last May to save time and cost for litigants in actions involving amounts up to $50. Its first day was a busy one—more than seventy cases having been scheduled. This ought to be a great help in relieving the other courts and be a benefit to the poor.

The textile strike still continues on its weary way. I think most of us pray daily that there will be no need in our locality to call out troops. It seems terrible that questions involving difficulties between responsible human beings cannot be settled without bloodshed. We hope for great things from the new board under Governor [John G.] Wynant.

A new discovery which may revolutionize telegraph and wireless devices now used is reported by the Research Engineers Division of the Radio Corporation of America. They call it the gateway to television and claim that whereas today it requires forty minutes to send pictures from New York to Chicago by the normal radio shortwaves, that only a fraction of a second will be necessary when tiny microwaves handle the pictures and printed matter through the services of booster stations.

From Washington comes the welcome news that the Comptroller of Currency, J.F.T. Connor, has reported to the Federal Advisory Council the approval of plans to reopen thirty-eight national banks with deposits of $52,896,000. Except for seven banks whose plans were disapproved, the report accounts for all of the fourteen hundred national banks which failed to open after the national bank holiday and seven banks subsequently added to the unlicensed list.

When I was young, long before I ever thought of doing anything in business or in the competitive world—which at that time belonged largely to men—I remember my grandmother admonishing me never to forget that "you are a lady." I am sure that same idea was dinned into many, many young women of my generation. And even today a woman must not be as aggressive about getting business, nor as persevering, if she does not want to have people feel that her attitude is not quite lady-like. She can never be as free and easy in her contacts unless she is an exceptional type who gradually establishes herself among the men she comes in contact with, and with whom she works as a good fellow who needs no consideration, beyond that accorded to men by each other. Some women resent this very much. But they might just as well make up their minds that they cannot have their cake and eat it too. If women are going to compete with men, they must either use their minds and insist on being equal in every way—and lose that something of glamour which surrounds women who are set apart behind certain restraints and reserves—or they must compete as women, using as part of their competitive armor that mysterious something which is so well described in [Stephen] Vincent Benét's *John Brown's Body* in speaking of the Southern lady:

> And always, always to have the charm
> That makes the gentlemen take your arm
> But never the bright, unseemly spell
> That makes strange gentlemen love too well.

I do not think that, as a matter of fact, women today in the professions and in business or in public life are trading much on this prerogative. They are trying, as far as possible, to disassociate themselves as workers from their personalities as women. On the whole I think this is a healthy attitude to take, and makes for better feeling in a competitive world. No woman can really reach a place of recognition unless she has actually earned that place. No amount of chivalry is going to place her there if she cannot "deliver the goods." Therefore, women might just as well make up their minds to keep their charm and their womanly personalities for their homes and to disabuse the minds of their competitors of the old idea that women are only "ladies in business."

This is even truer where it concerns women who are going into public life either as elective or appointive officials. They have learned that they must be themselves. They cannot assume an attitude or qualities which other people may think becoming to their positions. They must stand or fall on their own ability, on their own character as persons. A good motto is "Be Yourself," and your associates and the public in general will render the verdict as to whether that self meets with approval. Insincerity and sham, whether in men or in women, always fails in the end in public life.

# 8.

# "A Day in the White House"

*The Simmons Program*

Tuesday, September 25, 1934

ER: We cannot help being deeply sorry for Colonel and Mrs. Lindbergh that they have again to be harrowed by details which must be very agonizing to them. However, it is extremely valuable to have criminals realize that when the United States government undertakes to bring people to justice, they keep right on until this has been accomplished. I am told that men have been apprehended at the end of ten and twelve years. I feel this phase of this case should be stressed, for it cannot help but serve as a deterrent to other people who are tempted by greed to commit some similar atrocity.

Everyone must be happy that the textile strike has been settled and that the board appointed by the president has succeeded in gaining the confidence of both sides. The stretch-out system is one which really needs study and it is to he hoped that, since a settlement has been reached, the mill owners will take back all their employees.

The papers state that [United Textile Workers official] Mr. [Francis] Gorman has received certain protests from mill employees where mills have not as yet opened. There may of course be reasons why this is inevitable, but if that is so, the tone of Mr. Gorman's statement is so temperate and the Wynant Board seems to be working so well, I think we are justified in feeling hopeful of a better understanding and a final settlement of these difficulties between the mill owners and their employees.

The final result of the International Boat Races is still in doubt, both yachts having flown protest flags in today's race. We all of us hope that there will be general satisfaction with the decision of the committee and that the British sense of fair play will be matched by our own.

From Watertown, Massachusetts, comes a story of an amusing hobby. Frederick Gleason Richardson saves postmarks from all over the United States and he has unearthed some curiously named places in this country of ours. He has Coffee and Toast from Georgia and North Carolina; he has OK from Kentucky; So-So from Mississippi, and he has found towns for each of his own three names in the states of Illinois and Tennessee.

From Geneva comes a plea from James G. McDonald [League of Nations], high commissioner for refugees from Germany, telling the sad story of the exodus from Germany not only of Jews but of non-Jewish people as well. He appeals for help in rehabilitating these people in the countries in which they are now settling.

Ireland is a small country and a very serious condition exists there. A government survey just made on unemployment indicates that they have reached a peak and have 107,411 people without work. The situation in Liberia has become so acute that the United States has decided to make a fresh effort to bring order into that country. The movement to improve sanitary, sociological, and economic conditions has been at a standstill there since the League of Nations withdrew their offer of assistance last January. Mr. [Harry] McBride, who was once financial

adviser to the Liberian government, was sent out by our Secretary of
State, Mr. [Cordell] Hull, to inquire into the situation and is now on
his way home. The reason why we have stepped in is that most of the
other countries, after the League of Nations investigation, seemed to
agree that Liberia was our responsibility. We are so far away from it that
we have doubtless forgotten, but it was primarily with this country that
our original slave trade flourished, and those curious old Bible-reading,
psalm-singing sea captains who engaged in this trade are the ones who
are responsible for our present interest in Liberia.

From Tokyo, we are glad to see dispatches that the Soviet Union
and Japan are resuming their negotiations for the sale of the Chinese
Eastern Railroad. This agreement should improve Russo-Japanese relations and dispel some of the war clouds which have been hovering
over that horizon. From Paris and Zurich come two dispatches which
dovetail into each other. One is the information that the French Foreign
Minister, Louis Barthou, returned to Geneva to take up the delicate
business of finding a formula for an eastern European peace pact. While
in Zurich, the Women's International League for Peace and Freedom has
been meeting.

From Chicago comes the interesting item that the [meat] packers
have granted a wage increase of 8 percent, which will total $10 million
a year. The report as of June stated that employment in the packing industry was 101.4 percent of normal; the payroll, 87.2 percent; and the
average weekly wage was $21.82.

If the weather is favorable word comes from Detroit that Jean Pic-
card, who made the first [balloon] ascent into the stratosphere, will take
off with his wife at four a.m. on Thursday, hoping to reach a height of
61,000 feet in their balloon.

There is being carried on at present a drive to make people in general
drink more milk. In fact, one circular being sent throughout the schools
advocates a quart of milk a day per person. And milk is recommended

for those who do not wish to put on too much weight, for milk adds
fewer pounds than beer! In Atlantic City, the judges who passed on the
merits of twenty-three brands of beer at the convention of the New
Jersey Licensed Beverage Association must have put on several pounds
at least!

From Shanghai comes the story of a new tax. We really do not in
this country know what it is to be taxed. The Chinese understand the
art, and the last one imposed is a "good feelings" tax. It is supposed to
be devoted to supplying the provincial soldiers with food and clothing.
Aren't you glad you do not live in China?

Last winter there came to me a letter, and it ran somewhat like this:
"Dear Mrs. Roosevelt: Why do you take so many trips? Think of your
poor husband sitting at home, alone in the evening, with no one to keep
him company by the fireside." As is usual with such letters it was un-
signed. People seem to enjoy very much giving advice and yet do not like
to stand by it by adding their names. It occurred to me—and this belief has been strengthened since this letter—that there are a great many
people in this country who have not the remotest idea of the life which is
lived by the man who is elected to be president of the United States. Or
by his wife. Of course, it is obvious that the conditions in the country
as a whole, and personal preferences, make some slight change in the
lives of the individuals occupying the White House. But by and large,
they lead, administration after administration, very much the same kind
of life. In the first place, they carry a burden of work which is scarcely
understood by people throughout the country. The president and, to a
lesser degree, the head of every federal department, has practically the
entire day filled with appointments to see people, especially while Congress is in session. That means that the big volume of mail must be attended to in the late afternoon or evening or early morning. Speeches
must be written and any real thinking on troublesome subjects must be
done in these periods of so-called leisure. I have found, for instance, that

what exercise I hope to get must be over with by eight thirty a.m., when we breakfast. After that I cannot call a single minute of the day my own.

My husband always liked to have his breakfast in peace and quiet and not to see people until he had a chance to read his morning paper. But at times of stress even this rule is ignored and gentlemen come to confer from eight o'clock in the morning, and it is all he can do to get dressed and get over to his office. There is never a free evening. Evenings are times for conferences and work with one or two people over knotty problems, or for dictating. It is rare for either of us to go to bed much before twelve or one o'clock, and we have been working at our desks all evening long. Occasionally there is a movie after dinner. Even if you cannot have a rest in one way, at least your mind must get some change. But when the movie is over, back to his desk goes the president.

This routine is not just because the duties are what they are today, for every other president has found the burden a heavy one. I can remember personally back to Theodore Roosevelt's day, and he always went to work after dinner. There are stories of how both President and Mrs. Hoover worked, how engrossed Mr. Hoover was at all times and how he would even pass people without seeing them, his mind was so completely wrapped up in the questions before him. He hardly took time to eat, and certainly those who observed him doubted whether his mind, in the brief periods of relaxation which he allowed himself, ever left the difficult problems that had occupied it in office.

Mr. Coolidge was a methodical gentleman and lived his years in the White House in rather placid times, so that he had time for some of the rest which he had been accustomed to every day. But even at that, there was no time hanging heavily on his hands and there were many evening sessions. Nearly every president has to have some form of exercise, for a sedentary life spent largely at a desk requires that individuals have regular air and exercise if they are to keep well. President Wilson played golf. But I seem to remember stories that he worked early and late to pay for those hours spent on the golf course. And there were times when he could not get that amount of exercise and relaxation. Theodore Roosevelt had to be out of doors and took long rides and long walks and played tennis. But he was up early in the morning and often late at night.

So when you feel the impulse to wonder why the occupants of the White House do this or that, just remember that their lives are very different from the lives of the average individual who works hard from nine to five and may have still some housework or some chores to do when returning home but who goes to bed fairly early and who frequently has the choice of how the evening shall be spent. I think every occupant of the White House will tell you that their choice is rarely a free one.

# 9.

## "Peace Through Education"

*Americans of Tomorrow Program*
for the Typewriter Educational Research Bureau

Sunday, November 11, 1934, 7:45–8:00 p.m. (CBS)

Two months after she signed off for mattresses, Eleanor Roosevelt was recruited by the typewriter industry to comment on the education of "Americans of Tomorrow." A Sunday-evening radio program was created, and it premiered on November 11, 1934, on the CBS network. The commercial messages in the program promoted portable typewriters for schoolchildren in the months leading up to Christmas. ER made the broadcasts from New York, Washington, and Warm Springs, Georgia, where FDR had built a cottage and where he and other polio patients from around the world sought treatment.

ER's first broadcast focused on the power of education to promote peace in the world. ER had long been an outspoken critic of war and a proponent of international cooperation. In the 1920s she campaigned vigorously for pacifist causes such as American participation in the

League of Nations and the World Court. In the 1930s, as first lady, she spoke on behalf of the Emergency Peace Committee organized by the Quakers, the National Conference on the Cause and Cure of War, and other antiwar campaigns. In 1934, ER described herself as a "very realistic pacifist."[1] As Germany and Japan built up their war-making capacities, ER maintained that the United States had to consider becoming better prepared to defend itself. Over the next seven years, ER would struggle to balance her pacifist convictions with her need to support FDR and his administration's defense policies.

In one of the broadcasts in this series, ER came closer to endorsing the advertiser's product than in any of her other commercial programs. She noted that typewriters had their place in a modern classroom and might even make learning more interesting. While she did not encourage schools to buy typewriters, she gently rejected the potential disadvantages that might be raised by opponents. The typewriter ad campaign was at least modestly successful. On Christmas morning, nine-year-old John Forbes King banged out a note to ER—in all capital letters—saying, "I have listened to your broadcasts about typewriters for children. Santa Claus brought me one."[2]

(MUSICAL THEME: WILLIAM DALY'S ORCHESTRA)

ANNOUNCER: Ladies and gentlemen. We have the honor of presenting Mrs. Franklin D. Roosevelt in the first of a special series of broadcasts in which her subject will be "Americans of Tomorrow." Today, Mrs. Roosevelt will give you her Armistice Day message, a message of peace through education. This program is sponsored by the Typewriter Educational Research Bureau of New York City—an educational bureau supported by the manufacturers of Underwood, Royal, Remington, and Corona portable typewriters. These companies found a few years ago that with the perfection of the portable typewriter as a small, light machine which a child could easily operate, and which a student could carry, they were allied with the cause of education by millions of young fingers. They found that their service to America was greater than the mere making and selling of typewriters. They were helping American children to better citizenship. The Typewriter Educational Research Bureau has fostered an investigation of the uses and benefits of typewriters through independent educational authorities, and is bringing the facts of this modern educational tool to the parents and teachers of America. Before we introduce Mrs. Roosevelt, William Daly will conduct his orchestra in a favorite waltz from the Johann Strauss operetta *Die Fledermaus.*

(ORCHESTRA)

ANNOUNCER: Ladies and gentlemen, Mrs. Franklin D. Roosevelt.

ER: Good evening, mothers and fathers. I am glad to have the opportunity to speak on "Americans of Tomorrow" on this day. Sixteen years ago today the World War came to an end. In talking to you about education tonight, the first question that comes to my mind is: What have we done through education in these sixteen years to make war less possible in the future? The boy who was a baby when the World War ended is almost old enough to be a soldier himself. Do the boys and girls in high school today understand any better the causes of war? Are they any better equipped to analyze the situations which lead up to war, or can they get at the truth about conditions in their own country or in other countries any better than we could?

This much I think we have done. We have a much larger group of young people today who are actively interested in questions of government and who study government from the time they enter high school. The war spirit, however, is built up in a thousand different small ways from early childhood on. All children love to play at different phases of real life. Little girls love to play with dolls and dollhouses, because it seems to them like keeping house and having babies of their own. All little boys have been brought up on toy soldiers, primarily dressed in the uniforms of their own country, though frequently they have been supposed to learn something of history by playing with soldiers dressed as Romans and Greeks. Or if they are American children, in the traditional red coat of the English soldier—who tried to keep us under Great Britain's control. There was a time when Germany produced the most remarkable toy soldiers because in real life the army was a very important part of every German's existence, with the result that every small boy played with soldiers from his earliest childhood on.

We have also taught history in a way which has led every child to feel that military heroes are great figures in history. It is not until they are comparatively mature that young people discover that some of the most important people in the development of various countries never wore a soldier's uniform. The glory of war has been constantly emphasized and rarely the sordid side—the filth, the cold, the horror of wounds, and of slow death—these are all hidden behind a veil of comradeship and patriotism.

Many a man who came back from the World War, even to this day, has no great desire to talk about his experience. And yet our youngsters of sixteen still think that there is glamour and beauty about war. They are accustomed to a competitive world, to a world in which strife is always going on about them. They do not even play games for the mere pleasure of playing; they must strive to win at all costs. So that they are even tempted, now and then, to cheat in order to obtain the victory. This may be a fitting preparation for the type of uncontrolled competition which they sometimes find when they enter upon the business of earning a living. But it hardly makes one considerate of the rights of others. Though in schools we give lip service to the Golden Rule and talk about it rather pompously as we grow older, I wonder how many of us really live it, or expect these youngsters to govern their lives in accordance with it. We have taught our children in their history to accept things which our country has done without too close scrutiny into the ethics of their government. Until these things are changed we might as well realize that we have made no particular strides in changing the psychology which makes it possible to sweep a nation into war with little preparation and little thought.

Armistice Day should make us think primarily about the steps which we should take to teach our children what real patriotism is. It is obvious that we cannot disarm without the cooperation of the other nations of the world. But we can create good feeling. We can train young people to understand the people of other nations and to be fair and just in their dealings with these people. Perhaps we will have to set our own house in order first, and do away with some of the practices which our world of business has allowed to creep in. If we find this to be so, let us face the necessity and so do.

There is one sure way to change ethical standards, and that is by beginning with the young child and helping him as he grows older to have the strength to stand against certain temptations which have been too great for many of us in the past. We must be sure, in the first place, that we ourselves, as parents and as teachers, believe in the standards which we are teaching the children. And that we are not simply preaching to them an impractical idealism which we expect them to shed when they enter the practical world. We must, at least, strive to live up to the things which we teach them, as their safeguard in business, in politics, and in international relations. There are many young people today who find themselves confronted with a situation in all of these fields which they consider to show up their elders in a somewhat hypocritical light. They claim that had we lived up to the things which we are now teaching them, the world would have been a different place from what it is today and life for them might be far easier.

We must be sure that we teach not only by word of mouth but by example, and that we give our children the opportunity, during their school years, not only to learn reading, writing, and arithmetic, but show a real appreciation of the arts and sciences. And if possible, to develop any talent which they personally may have. For these creative activities may mean much in the greater leisure which we hope for in the future. A real knowledge and understanding of literature, not only because it is part of the curriculum, but for real enjoyment of books, will mean much to the future life of any child and to the culture of any country.

At the same time it is important that children grow up in an atmosphere of interest in public questions, and it is becoming increasingly evident that good government, particularly in a democracy, depends upon the interest and responsibility which every individual citizen is willing to shoulder. A child brought up in a home where they hear these questions discussed will take it for granted that he must, in time, take up his share of the responsibility and exercise his good citizenship through a knowledge of the issues at stake and of the people for whom he votes.

Teachers, mothers, and fathers are responsible for the developing of the characters of our citizens of tomorrow. If we are to have continued peace it will be through our own efforts. We do not want to bring up children who are afraid of war, horrible though war may be. We want to bring up children who have an understanding of the problems of the world, who have the ability to be fair and generous in their judgments and strong enough to stand by their beliefs and to work for peace in the same way that, in the past, we have worked to build up the material success of our nation and its defense when it was needed. Working toward peace is a slow process, it means changing human nature, changing the thought of nations, but we are the nation that can do it and the only way to begin is to begin!

ANNOUNCER: Thank you, Mrs. Roosevelt. Now William Daly and his orchestra, playing "Vilja" from *The Merry Widow*.

(ORCHESTRA)

(CLOSING ANNOUNCEMENT)

# 10.

# "World Court Broadcast"

Sunday, January 27, 1935, 10:45–11:00 p.m. (NBC Red Network)

During the 1920s, Eleanor Roosevelt was a leading advocate for American participation in the League of Nations and its Permanent Court of International Justice, or World Court. She continued the campaign as first lady.

The League of Nations was proposed after the end of World War I in 1918. The war caused a staggering number of casualties: more than 9 million combatants died and more than 7 million remained missing. President Woodrow Wilson and other League proponents argued that by voluntarily working together, the member nations could create a framework of collective security that would prevent the kind of massive bloodshed caused by modern, mechanized warfare. The World Court enjoyed popular support in America, but congressional opponents blocked legislation ratifying US involvement. They warned that belonging to the association would drag the United States into future European entanglements. Isolationists claimed that America had been thrust into the war by bankers and arms merchants out to make a profit. America should mind its own business, they said. Wilson's adversaries prevailed; in 1920 Congress voted against joining.

The League began operations in 1920 with forty-two member countries. The World Court opened two years later to hear disputes among nations. Pacifists such as Eleanor Roosevelt continued to crusade for the United States to join. When FDR was elected president in 1932, ER urged him to support the World Court legislation. Political pressure from isolationists made FDR reluctant to endorse the bill until 1935, when he finally backed the effort. The legislation had passed the House of Representatives but needed a two-thirds majority in the Senate.

On Sunday evening, January 28, 1935, leading figures for and against the World Court took to the national airwaves to rally the public. A Senate vote to join the Court was scheduled the next day. Fr. Charles Coughlin, the immensely popular radio priest from Michigan, urged listeners to contact their senators and voice their opposition to the international tribunal. "Today, whether you can afford it or not, send your senator a telegram telling him to vote 'No,'" Coughlin declared. "The World Court has demonstrated that it has no power to keep peace in the world." [1]

On NBC, Sen. Robert Rice Reynolds, a Democrat from North Carolina, gave a fifteen-minute speech against ratifying the World Court protocol. ER immediately followed with this fifteen-minute radio address in favor of the Court. The *New York Times* observed that it was the first time ER had "spoken so directly to the point of a matter of national interest being debated on Capitol Hill." [2]

The radio appeals, and a campaign against the bill by the Hearst newspaper chain, set loose a torrent of telegrams to Capitol Hill for and against the measure. Extra telegraph lines were set up and a double shift of operators worked through the night to handle the traffic. The Senate vote was delayed as supporters and opponents wrangled for leverage. Two days later, World Court ratification failed in the Senate by seven

votes. The United States never joined the League of Nations. It was re-
placed by the United Nations in 1945, for which ER was, again, one of
the nation's leading crusaders.

ER: Good evening, ladies and gentlemen and friends. I am speaking to
you tonight as a citizen and as a woman deeply interested in this question which you have heard discussed. I have listened with a great deal of
interest to the speech which was largely against the League of Nations.
We do not want to get into any other war. Nor did we want to get into
the World War. Flying, which so many of us do today, does not seem to
have made us grasp as yet how small the world is nor how dependent
we are on conditions in other parts of the world. I am frequently told
that you people who are listening to me tonight by your radios have no
interest in the World Court. If that is so, I am deeply sorry, for I love my
country and all its people, and I have a particular interest in the women
and the young people. I feel when you have thought of this question in
the light of today and of the future you will feel a deep interest in it too.
We are constantly told that the father of our country, George Washington, recommended no foreign entangling alliances. He was a progressive
for his day, and he knew what was good for our country in his day. But
with all his objection to entangling alliances, he did not spurn an alliance with France, which helped us to gain our freedom.

Today we have become a great nation, *the* creditor nation of the
world. Our tariffs have built competitive tariffs against us. It is becoming more difficult for us to trade with other nations. The lowered standards of living in other nations make it difficult for us to maintain our
own standards of living. We are a part of the world, no matter how
much we may wish that we could live unto ourselves alone. Now we
come to the question of joining the World Court. According to two of
our greatest jurists, the World Court is an independent body and not a
part of the League of Nations. We originated the idea of a World Court.

The Hague Tribunal was established because of our suggestion. It is an arbitral court. It will arbitrate difficulties between nations. In an arbitration, both sides give up something and the result is a compromise. The World Court is different because it is a court of law, and one of our very greatest jurists has said that what the world needs today is a body of international law; without it, we will never be able to settle our disputes by law and not by war. That is what the World Court was set up to do, and that is what it has been doing. We join it under an optional clause which allows no question concerning our interests to be submitted to the Court without our consent. All the other great nations, except Japan, who have joined the Court, have now signed a compulsory clause which obliges them to submit any question that is desired or brought up to the court.

The Court has decided forty-eight cases, rendering twenty-three judgments and twenty-five advisory opinions. One of the great American objections to the Court has always been its advisory jurisdiction, and yet these advisory opinions are one of the great uses of the Court, for by rendering these opinions in an early stage before the question is actually brought up for a judgment, many difficulties can be removed. Fifty-five nations have signed the Court's statute, forty-nine have ratified their signatures.

The United States signed in 1929 and is the only large country that has not ratified. The only real question before us now is whether we want to throw the weight of the United States behind a cooperative effort among the nations to develop international law and apply it to the settlement of international disputes, or whether we despair of finding any substitute for war.

And now a word as to the Norris Amendment. We all know that the president has full power by his initiative to involve us in war, but this amendment denies him a like power to keep us out of war by submitting the dispute to the World Court. This amendment provides, in effect, that one-third of the senators plus one may veto the submission of any dispute or question sent by the president to the Court for a peaceful disposition. The amendment was defeated, but it may have had an influence on your thought about the Court, and therefore I wish to speak of it tonight. It seems to me that we, the strongest nation in the world, cannot be afraid to take this step, to make this gesture in an effort to have questions settled by law and not by war. Is it really the spirit of our country's men and women, young and old, that they are afraid to join the World Court? I cannot believe it! The World War wasted billions of money and many, many human lives. After it, we had a short-lived prosperity and since then we have entered the depths of depression. We are finding our way out, but to say that any action which may help to prevent a recurrence of war is of no importance to the people of this country seems to me shortsighted. I remember the war well; I have looked on the acres of cemeteries in other countries where lie our boys and the boys of other nations. These dead are the result of war!

You may not care what happens in Europe or in Asia, but you feel here at home the result of anything which happens in other parts of the world. We cannot escape the reaction long. I have the greatest respect for the honored statesmen who are opposed to our entry into the World Court, though I differ with them for the reasons which I have given you. We cannot escape being a part of the world. Therefore, let us make this gesture for peace, and remember there was no World Court in 1914 when the Great War began. Since we have had a World Court, no nations have been forced into war by any decision of that Court, and some nations have been kept from what might have easily caused a war by these decisions.

I have not time to give you many instances, but just remember that Turkey and France might have come to war in the *Lotus* case, and the decision was rendered in favor of Turkey. And [Aristide] Briand, the great French statesman, though feeling ran high in France, said that he would gladly resubmit the case rather than go to war. Lately, Norway and Denmark submitted a question of sovereignty in deciding the Coast of Greenland, and it was decided again in favor of the small country, Denmark.

The Democratic Party put into its platform adherence to the World Court, and the convention ratified that platform, and the people—by their vote—ratified the fact that they believed that the party would keep its promises and that they believed in that party. I think we should have the courage to live up to our platform, and if you want to see the influence of your country on the side of peace, I beg of you to let your senators in Congress know that you want to join the World Court at once.

It will not make peace certain. It is only one step. But I believe in our desire as a nation to see justice done at home and abroad. And I make a special plea to the women of my generation who remember the World War and who desire to take any action they can to safeguard the youth of the future. I believe that the women of this country and the men are not afraid to make a gesture for peace. At least, I hope that this is so. Thank you.

# 11.

# "Making the Wheels Go
'Round in the White House"

*It's a Woman's World Program* for the Selby Shoe Company

Friday, March 15, 1935, 8:00–8:15 p.m. (CBS)

The first installment of Eleanor Roosevelt's radio show for the Selby Shoe Company caused the program's director to break out in a cold sweat. The broadcast originated from the roof garden of a hotel in Syracuse, New York. Some 350 people had been invited, but the room was too small to comfortably accommodate them, the sixteen-piece orchestra, the announcer, the technicians, and Mrs. Roosevelt. "Even today I marvel at the dexterity with which the slide trombone player managed to miss the back of the second violinist's head," director R. Calvert Haws later recalled.[1]

Haws had been fretting about the broadcast for weeks. He had been told that ER was hard to handle and that she discouraged supervision. He also learned that the first lady would arrive fifteen minutes before the live national broadcast and that there would be no rehearsal.

When the cue came, the band played, shoe manufacturer Roger Selby introduced ER, and she spoke for eight minutes about George and Martha Washington. One problem: her portion of the broadcast was supposed to fill nine minutes. "Nothing is more devastating momentarily to a radio director than to have a spare minute pop up," Haws wrote. Fortunately, the conductor was startled into action by the sudden silence, struck up the orchestra, and stretched the theme music to fill out the show.

Haws later discovered that no one had ever told the first lady that she needed to stay within an exact allotment of time on the radio. He also discovered that ER was perfectly happy to rehearse but no one had ever asked. "Other directors had been merely too much in awe of her to offer helpful suggestions," Haws recalled. He also declared that her performance at the microphone was much improved after his intervention.

ER was paid $4,000 for each of the eight programs of *It's a Woman's World*. ER's topics included whether a woman's place was in the home, keeping the White House going on a budget, and the life of a wife of a public official. She also answered listener questions that had been mailed in to her.

The national economy was still in depression in 1935. FDR created the Works Progress Administration (WPA) that year to employ millions of Americans in public construction projects. He signed the Social Security Act into law to combat poverty among the elderly. And with prodding from ER, he established the National Youth Administration to help jobless young people.

Overseas, Adolf Hitler had assumed total dictatorial power in Germany. The 1935 Nuremberg laws stripped Jews of most of their rights as German citizens. Fascist Italy invaded Ethiopia. Relenting to public opinion, FDR signed the first US Neutrality Act, which banned the export of arms, ammunition, or other war matériel to foreign nations at war.

This was the backdrop for ER's 1935 radio broadcasts. There were troubling headlines aplenty, but there were diversions, too. Bing Crosby and Bob Hope entertained on the radio. Fred Astaire and Ginger Rogers were dancing cheek to cheek in the movies, where Shirley Temple was "The Littlest Rebel" and Errol Flynn was "Captain Blood." When ER revealed on the radio that the White House needed repairs and had been providing shelter to mice, the *New York Times* reported the comments. In a separate article, the paper also observed that ER's radio earnings put her in the same salary bracket as the president.

ER: Over and over again, women ask me these questions: Just what *is* the daily routine in the White House of the president's wife? Are you always busy, as we are in our homes, or do you have hours of luxurious ease? I can readily understand that friendly curiosity, so for my first talk in this series I have outlined a typical day in the White House. Compared to many hurried days, this one would seem exceptionally calm and restful, but let's begin with the morning of that typical day.

Seven thirty and a cold morning! How I hate to get out of my bed and shut down the two windows between which my bed is placed. At last I screw up my courage, and with a leap I am out on the floor and hastily closing the windows. Then fifteen minutes of setting-up exercises, a cold sponge, and on with my riding clothes. Breakfast at eight fifteen in my sitting room. Or, if there are a number of children at home or guests in the house, in the West Hall. With my breakfast I read the morning papers if I am alone. Otherwise I look them over noting what I must read later on, then I run down and get into my car and drive myself out to the place where the horses are waiting. An hour's brisk ride along the Potomac, a bath on my return. If I am lucky, I will be at my desk between ten thirty and eleven o'clock.

Then comes the head usher, Mr. [Raymond] Muir, with his lists and plans for the day: when cars will be needed for the household, or for guests' going and comings, the arrangements for receiving groups and any number of other things for which he is responsible. The house-keeper, Mrs. [Henrietta] Nesbitt, must be seen each morning and told as nearly as possible how many guests there will be for meals during the day. She brings her menus for the day with her and any state functions are planned for in advance. After talking with Mrs. Nesbitt, then comes Mrs. [Edith] Helm, whose business it is to attend to the social side of the White House. She plans with me for the teas and musicals and state functions and makes sure that no one who should be asked is forgotten. This usually takes until twelve o'clock, when the real work of the day begins.

Individual interviews are usually given between twelve and one and two and three. This has not been uninterrupted time by any means. One or the other of the president's secretaries may have had to ask an important question about the president's plans which include me. Or members of my family and friends have perhaps called me on the tele-phone. My secretary, Mrs. [Malvina] Thompson, who has been with me for fourteen years, has been in and out with questions which have come to her either by telegraph, telephone, or mail, and which must be attended to immediately. After sorting the morning's mail, she brings me my personal mail unopened.

I shall give you a typical list of appointments and engagements. At twelve a representative of the Federal Emergency Relief Administra-tion who is in charge of the supervisors of social work throughout the country came in with her entire group of fourteen regional supervisors. We discussed the social-service work being done throughout the United States and the different problems of these women in different parts of the country.

At one thirty I changed my dress and went to a luncheon given by one of the cabinet wives. Back at the White House by three to receive the gentleman in charge of an investigation being made by one of our larger publications as to the attitude of youth on certain questions affecting policies at present before the country. At three forty-five, I received a lady who wished to give the president a very beautiful book which she had just finished. Unfortunately, the president was unable to receive it personally and therefore, I received it and expressed to her my husband's deep appreciation.

At four the entire group of cabinet ladies met to see some moving pictures of the work which is being done to remove the alley slums in the District of Columbia and to hear a talk from a housing expert as to what are the problems of housing in the District, with the object of trying to throw their influence to planning some useful project for the poor people of the District.

Five o'clock, a group of some ten people were received at tea. Usually at teatime my small grandchildren come in for a visit and occasionally they romp through the halls and make so much noise that it is a little difficult to hear what my guests are saying. In the meantime, certain people have come to me with questions as to the diplomatic dinner—about those who were ill and therefore not able to come to the dinner scheduled for that evening—the arrangements for a very gifted dancer who was to dance after dinner, where was she to dress, the change of costume must be made quickly. This last question was solved by building a dressing room with screens beside the stage in the East Room. This particular dinner was the largest ever given in the State Dining Room and it required much thought in having the tables arranged to seat the guests and still allow sufficient room for the butlers to serve.

By six I went in swimming with my husband. After that we dressed and were ready for our guests at eight, which included all the diplomatic corps and the secretary of state and Mrs. [Rose] Hull, with a few others entitled to be asked to this dinner. At the music afterwards some three hundred were added to the party. As a rule, the president does not wait to say good night to his guests, but I always remain until I have said good night to everyone. On this occasion, the president also remained, as he wished to be particularly cordial to his foreign guests.

This is typical of a day in the White House. Each day brings different questions and different problems but the time is allotted practically in the same way. Occasionally during the social season I cannot get time to ride in the morning and I am not able to look at any of the innumerable letters which I must personally answer, so when the day is too full after my guests have gone, another couple of hours in the middle of the night are devoted to doing the mail. Between one and two I usually get to bed at this time of the year.

# 12.

# "Keeping House on a Budget
in the White House"

*It's a Woman's World,* presented by the Selby Shoe Company

Friday March 29, 1935

ER: Being left alone for a few minutes in the green room of the White House with the chief usher, Mr. Ike Hoover, whom I had known as a young girl when my uncle Theodore Roosevelt was president, I turned to him and said, "Oh, Mr. Hoover, can you tell me anything about running the financial side of the White House?" Thus I faced the problem of the practical side of being in a house the size of the White House with its multitudinous public functions.

My predecessor, Mrs. Herbert Hoover, [no relation to Ike Hoover] had just very kindly shown me around the house with the aid of her housekeeper and secretary. I was feeling bewildered, but it was not the mere size which was so appalling but a sense of the traditions which would make it extremely difficult to make any changes, and the realization that there were endless rules and customs which would complicate housekeeping to a great degree.

I knew in a general way that servants' wages were paid for by the government and the number of servants was more or less prescribed by custom. But my husband had decreed that anything not absolutely necessary must be curtailed. I also knew that there was some kind of a fund for the official entertainments, but what it actually covered was a mystery.

Mr. [Ike] Hoover, who had doubtless explained it to many presidents' wives before, tried to make it clear to me. He told me that the president, out of his salary, pays for all the food for all the servants and the family with their unofficial guests. But anything which is an official entertainment, where both political parties were represented, *was* paid for out of a government fund, so that if the president invites a number of senators for breakfast or lunch, he must be sure not to have them all of one political faith, otherwise he will pay for the meal out of his own pocket!

And now for a little history of the White House. As you know, it was rebuilt in 1817, after the British had burned it. While numerous repairs and changes have been made since then, it is substantially the same building that was built in 1817. In a building over 117 years old, maintenance becomes a constantly increasing item. Strange though it may seem, pipes will leak at frequent intervals and rats and mice like old buildings, regardless of tradition. Two friends of mine sitting on the South Porch at breakfast one summer morning tried to reassure themselves that a squirrel ran across the floor and refused to admit until they were safely upstairs that they had seen a large and stout rat! These have since been exterminated but one has to keep constantly doing it!

An appropriation is passed by Congress covering the salary of all personnel—gardeners, guards, plumbers, carpenters, et cetera. The budget is made yearly, using the past experiences for estimating as closely as possible what will be needed for the maintenance of the house, the purchase of furnishings, rugs, linens, curtains, glassware, and china. As a matter of fact, there is usually little left out of the appropriation for refurnishing when the repair and maintenance items have all been taken care of. Practically every two years the White House has to be completely painted, and this is no task to be undertaken lightly and is a tremendous expense. We found, to our horror, the first year that we occupied the White House that the stone cornice was loose all the way around and for the safety of those who might walk below it was absolutely necessary that it should be repaired. Such things as that swell the cost of repair very rapidly and leave a very narrow margin for new things of any kind.

Anything bought for the White House in the way of linen is marked with the initials "U.S." on a shield. The White House china is marked with the president's shield and the silver is all of the same pattern and marked as it originally was in the president's house. We have found it necessary to buy inexpensive doilies and napkins and plated spoons for large entertainments, but this is a purely practical item and costs very little.

In addition to this yearly appropriation, Congress usually appropriates every four years a special fund so that an incoming administration may overhaul the house and make some definite improvements which need to be made. This fund is about the only one that one can really spend for replacing furnishings.

The height of the ceilings, and therefore the size of the windows, makes curtains and draperies an extremely expensive item and all the little economies practiced in any private home are practiced in the White House. Curtains are turned, rugs which are worn are sent to be rewoven or mended, and much darning and general repair work goes on in the sewing room on the third floor—all done by the maids, four in all, who have charge of the upstairs rooms. Two of the maids have been in the White House for a great many years.

The maintenance of the White House is under the supervision of the Department of the Interior, National Park Service. Repairs and furnishings, supplies, and payment of personnel are accounted for in the records of the Park Service.

The laundry of the bedrooms and the table linen is paid for as one of the items of maintenance, but personal laundry is paid for out of the president's own pocket in exactly the same way as food for the family and the servants and private guests. Stamps for personal letters, personal telegrams, and telephone calls are all paid for by the president and myself. Official communications must be signed by a secretary and the official mail must go out through the secretaries.

Any purchase for the White House, if it is a large one, must be handled through the Supplies and Warehouse Section of the National Park Service. Specifications are prepared and formal bids received and contracts awarded to the low bidders. For small purchases and emergencies, the chief of the Supplies and Warehouse Section telephones or sends one of his assistants to the various stores to obtain informal bids on the articles to be purchased. The president is authorized under the appropriation act to buy direct without securing bids or going through the Supplies and Warehouse Section, if he so desires. But as neither the president nor his wife have much time for personal shopping the more formal way is usually adhered to.

Immediately upon receiving anything for the White House, the article is duly recorded and entered in an inventory. All changes in White House property are accounted for on the inventory and presented annually to the president for his approval. This is in accordance with a provision in a section of a certain statute, 773–774.

You may see by this that housekeeping in the White House is a little complicated. When you buy any such things as a chair or table, or even new hangings for the formal rooms, it is customary to request the advice of the commissioner of fine arts. This is a wise practice, as it keeps these rooms harmoniously furnished, but it does add to the complications when so many people are consulted. Of course, gifts are frequently sent to the White House, either of furniture or china or hangings or rugs or paintings. These are, at once, referred to the Commission of Fine Arts, for if they are to be permanently placed in the White House, they have to be approved by the Commission of Fine Arts and accepted by an act of Congress.

Now as to the less formal duties of housekeeping, as far as possible, staple articles are bought wholesale and as the number of people in the White House is very great, a great many things are bought. In large quantities, a great many things are also sent in as presents, such as hams, game, fruit, et cetera. These are all passed on, of course, by the Secret Service and nothing is allowed to come to the president's table which has not been carefully gone over. A large storeroom houses the supplies and the housekeeper keeps a complete list of things as they are given out to the kitchen. She also tries to buy fresh things as far as possible from the markets around Washington and she does her shopping herself.

A very careful housecleaning is done during the summer months, besides a complete inventory of furnishings taken every June. One cannot be a lighthearted and happy-go-lucky housekeeper in the White House, for there is the weight of responsibility which always goes with handling anything which does not belong to you and which belongs really to the people of the United States. However, there is a certain pride in doing it all in a manner which will conform with the dignity of tradition, and at the same time preserve the simplicity which should exist in a democracy.

# 13.

# "What
# It Means to Be the
# Wife of the President"

*The Pond's Program*

Wednesday, April 21, 1937, 7:15–7:30 p.m. (NBC Blue Network)

Eleanor Roosevelt launched a new radio series for Pond's Cold Cream in the spring of 1937. The national economy had improved markedly since the depths of the Depression. American productivity rose above pre-1929 levels for the first time. Payrolls and stock prices had improved, unemployment was down. But it wouldn't last. Assuming that the recovery would continue, FDR slashed government spending and New Deal programs. By fall, the nation would slide back into deep recession.

The sound of war grew louder around the world. There was civil war in Spain, where Fascist forces bombed the city of Guernica. Japan invaded China, capturing Peking, Shanghai, and Nanking. The Nazis opened a concentration camp at Buchenwald.

ER's topics in the thirteen-week Pond's series would include audience favorites like a typical day in the White House and the rigors of official state dinners. But she would also discuss the problems of working women with her friend Rose Schneiderman of the Women's Trade Union League and the hardships of slum living with Ida Harris, the head of a group of mothers living in New York tenements.

The first lady made headlines when she explained in one program why she traveled so much. She said that if she stayed too long in the White House, she would lose touch with the rest of the world. In another program, she discouraged a George Washington University student from taking the so-called Oxford Peace Pledge to remain a pacifist in the case of war.

The issue of ER's radio pay became a controversy again in the summer of 1937. Hamilton Fish, a Republican member of the House of Representatives from FDR's home district in New York, was a relentless critic of the New Deal and the president. He accused ER of using loopholes to evade paying taxes on her radio work. As always, ER maintained that the $3,000 she got from Pond's went to the American Friends Service Committee. What ER did not disclose was that her radio agents typically got a $500 to $1,000 cut for each broadcast. The Treasury Department approved of ER's arrangement and the congressional committee investigating tax avoidance eventually dropped its inquiry into ER's finances.

ER often liked to have guests on her program. Sometimes she asked the questions; sometimes the guest did. On the program about being the wife of the president, ER was joined by Genevieve Forbes Herrick, whom ER referred to as Geno, a former *Chicago Tribune* reporter who had covered many of ER's White House press conferences, which were restricted to women reporters.

On one of the Pond's broadcasts, ER's guest was her daughter, Anna Roosevelt Boettiger. They interviewed each other on the proper ways to raise a girl in the twentieth century. ER would not have claimed to be an expert on this subject. Her own troubled childhood in a patrician family had ill prepared her for motherhood. ER and FDR had six children, five of whom lived to adulthood. ER left much of the child-rearing to a series of nannies and caregivers. ER later regretted her maternal ineptitude and the resulting struggles her children endured.

ANNOUNCER: This is Virginia Barr of the Pond's Company speaking from Washington, DC, and bringing you Mrs. Franklin D. Roosevelt. Tonight, in beginning this series of broadcasts, Mrs. Roosevelt talks informally about what it means to be the wife of the President. First, let me take just a moment to speak of the coronation. In a recent issue of *Life* magazine, there were pictures of beautiful women who will take part in the coronation social activities. On two pages, there were five women shown: a daughter of an earl, a sister of an earl, [and] wives of a baron and a baronet. Now, of these five English beauties, four use Pond's Cold Cream. So many English women use Pond's it has become the biggest-selling cold cream in England. Remember this when you're wondering what to do for your complexion. Follow the same method used by English and American beauties for refining the skin and keeping away signs of age. Cleanse and invigorate your skin night and morning the easy, effective Pond's way. Begin tomorrow. Get a jar of Pond's Cold Cream in the morning. Now, it's my great privilege to present Mrs. Franklin D. Roosevelt.

ER: Tonight I want to tell you a little of what it means to be the wife of the president. And I'm just going to talk it over here, for you, with Mrs. Genevieve Forbes Herrick—a very charming young lady whom I came to know soon after I first arrived at the White House. She used to be well known as a reporter on the *Chicago Tribune*. She and her husband are now living in Alexandria [Virginia], where she is writing a monthly feature for the *Country Gentleman*. Now, Geno, is that chair perfectly comfortable for you?

GH: Yes, it's fine, thank you. I wonder if you'd say, Mrs. Roosevelt, that being the wife of the president means being a very busy lady?

ER: Someone wrote me a letter recently in which she said in sport, "You may think you are useful to poke your nose into so many things. You are really America's first nuisance."

(LAUGHTER)

GH: How did you like getting a letter like that?

ER: I was very much amused. My family and I have laughed over it and I've even used it in a few speeches I've made.

GH: One of the things I've discovered about you, Mrs. Roosevelt, is a very keen sense of humor. Do you think a sense of humor is essential for a first lady?

ER: Well, I think if you can see the funny side of some things, it's easier now and then. For instance, the day a lady wrote me that if I would stay at home and attend to the housekeeping and not run around the country so much, she would not have soiled her white gloves on the stair rail which leads up from the lower floor to the East Room. I might have taken it really seriously and made my household unhappy, but knowing that the stair rail is wiped on an average of every fifteen minutes during the period when visitors are allowed in the White House, it struck me as extremely amusing that I should personally test the cleanliness of it. People do not realize the conditions that prevail in a house of this type and consequently cannot appreciate that it cannot be run exactly as your own house would be.

GH: I didn't meet you until after you came to Washington, and I've often wondered just what you thought when Mr. Roosevelt was elected for the first time in '32.

ER: Geno, I was terrified. One of my children was at the campaign headquarters that night. He came up and asked me the same question. If I'd dared to tell the truth then, I'd have told him what I've just told you.

GH: Why were you so terrified? When Mr. Roosevelt was governor of New York, didn't you get used to such a position?

ER: Four years in Albany were relatively simple. The White House, I knew, would be very different. To begin with, Albany was fairly near home. I would have to leave that. There were so many people I was fond of and with whom I worked; they couldn't all go with me. My time was taken up with so many interests that I'd have to curtail. And my privacy—I couldn't imagine what would become of that. I even remember wondering if I was going to be able to drive my own car.

GH: Well, you've been able to do that, haven't you?

ER: Well, yes. But one old gentleman I met up in Maine didn't think I should.

GH: What did he say?

ER: He said he didn't believe I was Mrs. Roosevelt because if I were, I'd have a chauffeur. He said his wife had always told him if she were living in the White House she'd have a chauffeur and the most expensive make of car.

GH: Well, Mrs. Roosevelt, you've kept right on doing things. How have all your fears worked out?

ER: I lost some of them when I decided that I'd be lost if I pretended to be anything I was not. Of course, that applies to everyone in any position. You must retain your natural self. If you don't, people whom you meet won't be themselves. They will think of you as a personage, not as a person. In realizing that, you see, many fears could be discarded. The household, the increase in mail, the more formal entertaining didn't really trouble me. But the realization of how much of it there'd be appalled me.

GH: You have quite a few people at the White House with whom you've worked before, haven't you?

ER: Yes, and I don't know what I'd do without them. There is really too much for one person to do. And if you have a few people you know can do things without supervision, you're lucky indeed. The greatest danger, from my point of view, is that many of them are so ready to be helpful and shield me from contact with the ordinary difficulties and activities of daily life that I might become a helpless individual. As an example, Mr. Ike Hoover, who was then head usher, informed me that it was not the custom for either the president or his wife to run the elevator. I had to be quite insistent before I was allowed to do it myself, in spite of the fact that I told him that I had worked a similar elevator in our house for years and that I could still do it.

GH: With so much to do at the White House, how do you find time to be away as much as you are?

ER: I think being out and around the country is just as important, more so sometimes, than some of the things I do in the White House.

GH: Why is that?

ER: If I stayed in Washington all the time, I'd lose touch with the rest of the world. I might have a less crowded life but I would begin to think, perhaps, that my life in Washington was representative of the rest of the country, and that is a dangerous point of view.

GH: What's the greatest satisfaction in being the president's wife? Or what do you enjoy the most?

ER: I'd say the sense of enlarged vision. Because you can see the nation as a whole, through individuals you meet from every part of the country. Also the ability the position gives you to do helpful things for a great many people. Take the little girl, for instance, who because I was so prominent in public, wrote and told me she had never been able to walk straight. Through the kindness of my friends in the orthopedic hospital, she was put through the necessary operations. After ten months in a plaster cast she came out as straight as any other child. She is now earning her own living.

GH: Meeting so many, don't people tend to become all alike to you?

ER: On the reception line it's hard to get more than just a casual impression. But I meet so many others who have something definite to tell me, both at the White House and around the country. Through such meetings I know those people as individuals. I know their lives. One day a woman stopped me as she went past me in the receiving line and said, "May I talk to you for a minute afterwards? I am trying to make my living as a farmer and I need some help." She came back afterwards and told me the familiar story of farm loans, drought, poor crops, et cetera. Between us we tried to work out some of the difficulties with the proper government agencies and I learned a great deal from her and it helped me to understand similar conditions throughout the country.

GH: What is the greatest drawback to being a president's wife?

ER: I think it's the fact that you have to think of what you do not as a private citizen but as a public personage. In private life you can be yourself, always. Those who know you will understand. But what you do of a public nature will be seen not only by friends who know you but by many people who will be affected by what you say or do without the background of knowledge of you, yourself. So you cannot count on a correct interpretation. For instance, a great many people may think that your interest in a certain thing is because of some political reason, whereas anyone who had known you would at once realize that that interest had been yours for many years.

GH: Do you think being the wife of a president changes a woman?

ER: No, I don't think it does inside. It changes your method of thinking to a certain extent, but it doesn't change you as a person at all.

GH: In being the wife of a president, what does that mean to your private life? Where do you get time for it?

ER: You have very little time. But you plan for such things as are important to you. You do what you feel you must do to retain your indi-viduality. Some people say they can get along without outdoor exercise. I feel that's necessary and will find time for it during the day even though it may mean I work far into the night. I feel it's important to get away from the White House and back to people who don't treat me as a personage. That's why I arrange my time so as to get away and be with old friends now and then. But Geno, before we get into our other questions, Virginia Barr has a word to say, and then we'll continue our talk.

(MIDDLE COMMERCIAL)

ER: Mrs. Herrick thinks I should tell you a little of what it means to run a presidential household.

GH: What about clothes? Do you have to have a new dress for every occasion?

ER: Oh my, no. But I have to have a great many more than I sometimes think I need. In the winter, with the increased entertaining, I have to have more dresses. This year I had new inauguration clothes, but if it were not for the many photographs one could wear clothes longer.

GH: Do you have any set time for going to bed?

ER: I never get there before eleven and frequently it is three a.m.

GH: And then up again at a quarter to eight?

ER: Oh, yes.

GH: How do you feel about the publicity that follows you so much?

ER: The essential publicity of public appearances concerns me very little. But other types of publicity concern me a great deal, not only for myself but for members of my family. Young people hate to have every move recorded and I myself very often feel that the people can hardly be interested in some of the things which are written.

GH: Do you write all your own things?

ER: Yes, I dictate every word which appears over my signature. I've been told that I have a ghostwriter, but there are no skeletons in my desk.

GH: What's the funniest thing that's happened to you?

ER: I don't know whether I think this is as funny as it is natural, but I made some purchases in a New York department store and gave my name and address as Mrs. F. D. Roosevelt, R-O-O-S-E-V-E-L-T, The White House, Washington, DC. The girl wrote quickly and, without looking up, said, "Any room number?"

(LAUGHTER)

ER: Now, Geno, I know we could go on forever but I must go home, for we have people staying in the house and one rule is that the president is not kept waiting, and he expects dinner at seven forty-five. In closing, I should like to say to all who are listening that we will welcome any suggestions or questions you want to send in. I really can't acknowledge your letters though, and we can't give any assurance that your questions will be answered in the ensuing broadcasts, but we will do our best. And if you do write, would you please address your letters to the radio station to which you're listening?

Next Wednesday I'll be back again to describe a typical day in the White House. I'm going to select a recent day and then Mrs. Thompson and I will tell you all about it. You know I feel that the White House is your house, and in this way I hope you will feel that you're sharing a day with me there. Good night.

(COMMERCIAL)

(CLOSING ANNOUNCEMENT)

# 14.

# "Education of a Daughter for the Twentieth Century"

*The Pond's Program*

Wednesday, May 5, 1937

ANNOUNCER: This is Virginia Barr of the Pond's Company, speaking from Seattle, Washington, and bringing you Mrs. Franklin D. Roosevelt. Tonight, Mrs. Roosevelt is going to give us her ideas on the education of a daughter for the twentieth century.

(COMMERCIAL)

BARR: And now I have the great privilege of presenting Mrs. Franklin D. Roosevelt!

ER: Good evening. As I am in Seattle now, visiting my daughter, Anna Roosevelt Boettiger, and her family, I asked her to join me tonight and together we are going to discuss for you the education of a daughter for the twentieth century. I, from the point of view of educating Anna, and Anna, from the point of view of educating her [own daughter] Eleanor.

AB: That's right, Mother, and don't forget to speak of her always as Eleanor. She doesn't like "Sistie" anymore.

ER: Yes, I'll be very careful.

AB: Well, in talking about education, I often wondered how you picked the various phases of mine.

ER: I tried to pick out the things which meant most to me. My grandmother, who brought me up, thought of all women as wives mothers, and adornments to society. I didn't want to restrict you to that field. I had a faint inkling that you would have to meet different circumstances than had fallen to my lot. I wasn't perfectly sure what your preparation should be, but I believed any aptitudes you showed should be given an opportunity to develop. From your point of view, Anna, what do you feel was the most useful part of the education you received?

AB: The most useful? Well, I think it was the development of my bump of curiosity.

ER: I'm glad to hear you say that. What do you feel developed it most?

AB: Why, you and Father. You made me feel there is so much in the world that not a second should be lost learning all about it.

ER: I think I remember several seconds, and even minutes, which you thought could be missed when it came to learning various subjects.

AB: Oh, that was in school, Mother. But at home, I was terribly curious about everything, except maybe learning to play the piano. If I remember rightly my chief interest lay in hiding in the kitchen closet when my music teacher was about to arrive.

ER: I never knew that, Anna. But as you hated to play the piano, I think it's interesting that you make Sistie, I mean Eleanor, do it. You'd better explain that a little.

AB: Oh, she *wants* to learn. She has a good ear and she also plays in her school harmonica band.

ER: I know, but tell me this. If she didn't want to learn, would you still make her?

AB: No. Not if it was only so she could play little pieces for company. But yes if it would help her appreciate music and get more fun out of playing later on.

ER: Now, Anna, back to that curiosity of yours.

AB: Well, one thing, I know I was terribly curious about people. I still am.

ER: Your father and I made a point to have you with us a great deal. And to give you every opportunity to meet all types of interesting people. I think that's an important part of anyone's education, for nowadays a person has to work with so many different types of people that it's never too early to start getting used to them. And another result of a child's being familiar with people is the development of poise. They learn to be at ease with others, know how to be themselves—natural at all times. That will be one of their greatest assets all their lives.

AB: I remember when I was eighteen I toured New York State with the women's division of the Democratic State Committee. I had to keep all the schedules and all the accounts, and get along with everybody on the tour. If I hadn't learned about people before I went on that trip, I would have been lost. Then when I branched out into other types of work, such as the Girl Scouts and later into radio and writing, I found out again how important knowing human beings is as a background.

ER: Another thing that I think mothers are interested in today is the reading their daughters do.

AB: I wanted to find out what was between the covers of almost every book I could lay my hands on. And I think that today my understanding of a great many things is traceable to the historical background I got from reading all sorts of books.

ER: It was a good thing I didn't censor your reading. It seemed to me that to be turned loose in a library, as I had been when I was a child, was the best way of gaining knowledge. If you happened on a book that was unsuitable to your age, you simply would not understand it, but it would do you no harm. I may be wrong about this theory but it seems to have worked with you.

AB: Well, I'm going to use the same theory with Eleanor.

ER: She isn't much of a reader yet, is she?

AB: Just now her chief interests are tomboyish rather than bookish. Playing cops and robbers is her favorite pastime when school is out.

ER: There's another thing, Anna, that bothered me as a girl. I had an inferiority complex, which so many children suffer from.

AB: It took me a long time to get over mine and I think that was your fault.

ER: Really? Why?

AB: Well, I never felt I could be as capable and interesting as you and Father were.

ER: I have heard many young people say that about their elders. I have come to believe that one of the essentials of education is developing a sense of self-confidence. If only our companionship could have developed as freely when you were little as it did later on. I would have probably understood a great deal more. You are doing a better job with your child.

AB: That's nice of you, Mother. But how do I know how she'll feel about it when she grows up?

ER: That's so, but perhaps she'll feel as we do now. I don't think of you only as a daughter but as my best friend.

AB: You're quite right, and companionship is one of the fundamentals of education. To develop this companionship with my daughter today, I feel that I can never allow myself to go stale, never lose my perspective, sense of humor, or the ability to put myself in the other fellow's place—in my daughter's place. But there are other fundamentals too.

ER: If you mean the R's: readin,' ritin' and 'rithmatic, I think they are a necessity. But there is one more fundamental, and that is to learn to think for oneself and to know where and how to look up information and to concentrate on your study.

AB: I've got one more important than that: seeing *why* you should learn those facts. I know any number of children who would be bright students if they could only get a good answer to why they have to learn. History dates, for instance. And when I was in school the art of darning seemed so useless. I remember being handed a perfectly good piece of cloth with a hole cut in the middle of it and being told to darn it. Well, I did. But then when it was approved they cut it all out and made me practice darning a bigger hole.

ER: (LAUGHING) Oh, I know just how impatient you got, but it's very essential for little girls to know how to darn.

AB: Well, I learned soon enough without studying it at school. What do you think now, Mother, about making a daughter do things which are good for her but which she doesn't want to do?

ER: You ought to let me ask *you* that question. But my answer is that I still think it's important to learn obedience. When I was young, no explanations were ever made to me. But today I think they should be made. Children get out on their own sooner now and they have to be trusted to decide things for themselves. That is why I think mothers should explain the reasons behind their direction, whenever possible. At the same time, a child should know that if it is told to do something, it must do so, even if the reasons can't be explained until later on.

AB: I've heard you mention self-discipline very often, Mother.

ER: I know you have, and I think it's most important. Today there is more freedom than ever before. Almost any path is open to girls, both into the field of knowledge and of experience. We have to put great emphasis on trustworthiness and a child's knowledge of right and wrong. The only safeguard we can rely on is self-discipline. Now, Anna, I have some questions I want to ask you, but first Virginia Barr has a word to say.

(MIDDLE COMMERCIAL)

ER: Anna, you are in a different generation, and your Eleanor will be in still another. What specific plans are you making to help her meet situations which you feel will be different when she is grown up?

AB: I think that my answer to that can be pretty close to yours, though different in one respect. I think, possibly more than you thought, that my daughter should be prepared for great changes. I don't think that she, or any other girl, should feel that the picture from which they learn their lessons will be the same as the one in which they meet actual experience.

ER: That sounds as if you were advocating adaptability.

AB: That's it exactly.

ER: Well, you're perfectly right. I know our generation didn't think of that so much when I was educating you. Of course, I think every girl should learn how to make and run a comfortable home. She should know before marriage the rudimentary care and bringing up of children. But besides that she should have some training that will enable her to earn her own living if necessary.

AB: But Mother, don't you think it's sometimes hard for a girl who doesn't have to work to understand why she should strive to fit herself to lead a useful life?

ER: Oh, no, I don't think it should be hard for any girl to see why she should lead a useful life.

AB: Well now, I don't mean it that way. But take an eighteen-year-old girl whose father earns enough to support her at home, it might be hard to explain to her why she should train for a job.

ER: You remember that young woman with the little boy whose husband was an aviator? They lived in various South American countries. Her greatest asset was foreign languages. But she had no training, no experience in any line of business. Yet when her husband was killed she had not only herself but her small son to support.

AB: Is that why you tried to give me some training?

ER: Yes, but in line with the interests you showed. I felt that as one of the things you liked was the country, you might as well learn a little about farming, and so I insisted you take those agricultural courses at Cornell.

AB: I know now that was a good idea. But I didn't like it then. I was having too good a time. Do you remember that day we drove up to Geneva, New York, to the experiment station?

ER: Yes, you were so put out by the whole idea that you wouldn't speak to me for the entire seven-hour drive.

AB: But Mother, what about the girls who have no particular talent?

ER: I think if they are wise, such girls will fit themselves for some line of work which they can use if necessary. And in time they may develop individual interests. Now, Anna, you know this better than I. What do you want for your daughter in life?

AB: What a question! I think I'd say freedom from any sense of superiority or inferiority to any group of people. And knowledge that she gains much from everyone she meets. And a sense of values that will help her to be tolerant, useful, and happy.

ER: That's the twentieth-century answer, and I like it. I think the girl will be well educated to live in our world. I think if my grandmother had been asked what she wanted for her daughter she *might* have answered simply: "A good husband!" (PAUSE)

Now Anna and I must leave you to go home and see the daughter that she is educating for the twentieth century. Next week, I'm going to be back in New York and when I talk to you from there I am going to have a very dear friend with me, Miss Rose Schneiderman. We are going to talk over some of the phases of the life and some of the problems of the working woman today.

As I told you, if you have any questions or suggestions, I should love to get them. And we will try our best to work those which will be of the greatest general interest into our broadcast. If you want to write, just address your letters in care of the station to which you are listening. Good night.

# 15.

# "Problems of Working Women"

*The Pond's Program*

May 12, 1937

ER: Good evening. Here I am back in New York, after flying all the way across the continent and back on one of the most delightful trips I have had in several years. This evening I have the pleasure of introducing to you a friend, Miss Rose Schneiderman, who has come to talk over with me some of the problems of the working woman today. Miss Schneiderman is the president of the Women's Trade Union League and the secretary of the New York State Department of Labor. She came to this country from Russia as a young girl, and was thrown almost immediately on her own resources. Her father died and she and her mother were compelled to earn the money to support a large family. Rose Schneiderman has worked under all sorts of conditions. Yet she has not become bitter or self-centered. She has never lost her innate sense of fairness and her desire to do what is right for everyone she can help.

RS: Thank you, Mrs. Roosevelt. As I've been sitting here, I've been thinking of the first time I met you.

ER: That was in 1919 in Washington, wasn't it?

RS: Yes, it was. And after that you offered to help with those educational courses we were giving at the New York Women's Trade Union League. One of my most vivid impressions of you is pouring cups of cocoa and passing cakes to fifty girls whom you met every Thursday night, reading aloud to them and discussing the literature over the refreshments you always brought along.

ER: I still look back on those evenings as some of the most valuable evenings I've ever spent. Because, as we talked together over those cups of cocoa, I learned more about the lives those girls led, and their problems, than I could have in any other way. Without that experience, I should be lost now in coping with some of the situations I hear about almost every day. But now, Rose, that was yesterday. What about today?

RS: Today we know that the time is past when we argue whether a woman *should* work or not. Because, you see, now women have become absolutely indispensible to our industrial scheme.

ER: Well, that's your opinion, Rose. But you ought to read some of the letters I get. People write me all the time saying the whole unemployment problem could be solved by taking women out of the labor market.

RS: Well, the girl who works today doesn't work for pleasure. She works, in most cases, because she has to. There may be an invalid mother home, or three small sisters and no father or mother. And then she still wants a husband, a home, and children. But to get married, it may be up to her to supply part of the family income. Before the Depression, it was quite customary for a girl to leave her job when she got married. But, now, it's more likely she'll leave the office or factory Saturday noon, get married, and be back on the job Monday morning.

ER: That's true. Marriage for many a girl today means the beginning of a dual life. She has two responsibilities, that of her home and that of her job.

RS: Working out those two responsibilities successfully is one of the working woman's chief problems. I, personally, don't think that either has to suffer because of the other. In fact, sometimes each may benefit.

ER: I know one case in which the wife's working *saved* the family situation. She was never domestically inclined, and while during the first year of her baby's life she took extremely good care of her, she chafed at having to accept everything from her husband without making any financial contribution herself. The relationship grew strained. Finally she went back to work. She earned enough money to buy her own necessities and help run their home. The conversation of an evening in that home is far more pleasant than it used to be. That family is growing together instead of apart.

RS: You know, our labor statistics show that the majority of married women who work contribute the major part of their earnings to the support of dependents—children, parents, unemployed relatives.

ER: That spikes the statement I am sure you have heard many times, that women take jobs away from men and spend the money on clothes, beauty parlors, and pleasures.

RS: Oh, yes, I know. Some of their money does go for that. But why shouldn't it? There's no reason why our production methods shouldn't benefit our girls. It would be a waste of our economic resources if we didn't use the clothes we produce. And another angle on that: I know of the case of one factory foreman who told one worker that if she couldn't make a better appearance on the job, she'd get fired.

ER: Neat, nice-looking clothes definitely contribute to the efficiency of a worker. Now, Rose, I've been carrying on a pretty spirited correspondence with a woman from a state where there is some legislation proposed for the protection of women in industry. She herself is evidently a professional woman. Now, here's one of the things she says: "We are worried to death about a bill to limit women but not men to forty hours a week." You see, Rose, her contention is that it is unfair to limit women and not men. She forgets that men, being better organized than women, have already made many of these arrangements rather successfully for themselves.

RS: Few people realize how difficult it is for unskilled women to organize [a labor union]. They frequently look on their employment as temporary. They're looking for some man to come along to take care of them. Also they're afraid if they organize they may lose the jobs they need so desperately.

ER: That's true. Now, this lady I've been corresponding with adds this: "Somehow I cannot shut out of my heart a little resentment against those men who are so blithely attempting to take from me the right to compete with any competitor for the best living I am capable of making."

RS: I'd like to answer that.

ER: I'd like to have you.

RS: In all seriousness, I am not interested in maximum hours and minimum pay for professional women. They are trained and educated and can jolly well take care of themselves. Let's face facts as they are. Of course I want the best possible working conditions for all people, men and women, and it's obvious to me, as it must be to you, Mrs. Roosevelt, that when the working conditions of women are bettered, those of men automatically rise too. You see, when women work long hours and for next to nothing, they are not only competing against each other but are pulling down the wages of their men folks. The women who are working in factories who have home responsibilities, too, need improved conditions most. There are very few men who go home at the end of the day to do the housework.

ER: Oh, I've known some who have.

RS: Oh, yes, of course some do. But they only do it in an emergency. They drop it as soon as they can.

ER: That's so. And I don't think there's any question that a woman who works to give her children the necessities and some of the advantages of life should have her workday limited to eight hours. She has to provide her child with companionship. She has to oversee her home, for no home can run without supervision. I know one woman with six children to bring up. Her husband's wages were not sufficient to give the children the clothes and educational advantages she was determined they should have, so she worked on the night shift in a mill. She was strong and sturdy, and for a time things went well, although I think the sum total of the sleep she got was only four hours a day. After a while she found that her children were getting out of hand. The eldest boy was in trouble with the police. If that woman could have worked an eight-hour day, she could not only have provided the necessities but could have given her boys and girls the companionship and guidance they needed.

RS: I know any number of cases just like that.

ER: Of course you do. But now, Rose, before I go on to the other questions I want to ask you, Virginia Barr has a word to say.

(MIDDLE COMMERCIAL)

ER: What do you think, Rose, is the most vital question facing working women today?

RS: I would say getting over their economic inferiority complex. I think girls should realize that they are just as important to the nation industrially as men are. I've known many women who have felt they could never hold down a job, and even when they find they can, they carry this feeling of inferiority into business and industry and are willing to work for much less pay. You know, in unskilled work, women get one-third less for the same work men do.

ER: Like everything else, working conditions change. What would you say is the most significant change going on before our eyes today?

RS: That's a large question. But there is one stage of evolution we're going through right this minute. When immigration was unrestricted, the American girl went into "business." That is, she worked in an office. We depended on the immigrants for the factory work and domestic employment. Now an increasing number of American-born girls are needed and are going into these fields.

ER: Many women consider housework demeaning, which it is not, of course. But I don't believe that American girls are going to be willing to go into domestic service unless better working conditions prevail.

RS: I think household workers have a right to expect a room of their own, some chance for that privacy which we all must have. Hours are excessive, especially when a girl is on call from six in the morning until the last member of the family goes to bed at night.

ER: And there's another point in that connection. All women who are going to employ labor in the home, or in any other way, should know what it means to work themselves. If not, they can never be good employers.

RS: Here's something I'd like to ask you. What about the girl who stays at home who doesn't go to work?

ER: I sometimes think that the *wife* who stays at home, and carries on all the work in the household, should be paid a definite salary. She earns it, without any question. Any girl who is needed at home has a job just as surely as the girl who operates a machine in a factory. If she is not needed at home, I think she loses out by not working. I think she limits her contacts with other human beings and her whole personality suffers. Now, Rose, how would you answer this question? Do you think men really resent women in industry?

RS: Emotionally, I think they do sometimes. But they need them just the same. But, Mrs. Roosevelt, can you imagine what would happen if close to 11 million working women in the United States suddenly quit their jobs and just waited for the men to support them?

ER: Well, then the men *would* resent them! In solving all the problems of the world, men and women must work together. When they have worked side by side in the factory, for example, they understand each other better. I am convinced that often the girl who has worked is a more capable wife. She is more valuable to herself than the girl who has never known the give-and-take of the working world. (PAUSE)

Now Miss Schneiderman and I must leave—she to go to a meeting of the North American Housing Exposition, and I am going to the theater again. Two plays in one week—an orgy which I haven't indulged in for a long time. Next Wednesday I am going to talk to you from Washington, and I'm going to tell you a little about the White House, some of the interesting and amazing things connected with it that I have learned only through living there. Good night.

# 16.

# "Life in a Tenement"

*The Pond's Program*

Wednesday, June 23, 1937

ER: Good evening. In the studio with me this time is Mrs. Ida Harris, who was born and brought up on the Lower East Side in New York. Mrs. Harris knows firsthand just what living in a tenement means. She's brought up her family there. And in recent years she has added to her family duties the job of being an active member of the League of Mothers Clubs. Now she is president of that organization of tenement mothers, all of whom are determined to achieve better homes for their families. When I was living more in New York and doing social-service work there, I knew well indeed the districts which Mrs. Harris knows. Many is the time I have visited people there. And this evening we are going to tell you something about living in slums. We hope you will see why we are working so hard to make life in them better. I remember, Mrs. Harris, it was just about a year ago that you came to the White House with a petition for the president.

IH: Yes, Mrs. Roosevelt. A committee of three members from the League of Mothers Clubs went to Washington to bring a very unique document to the president. It was a book of pictures that our mothers had taken in New York for the president to look at. It showed you the conditions of how the people live, the hallways, the public toilets, the sinks, and some of the people. You could see in the women's faces what they are enduring in those houses.

ER: The president spoke of that document. It was an extremely forceful way of presenting your case.

I shall never forget my first visit, as a young girl, to a tenement. I was going to see a woman who had worked for my mother. She had married, had five or six children, and was very ill. I climbed to the third floor. The hallways were dark, the stairs rickety, and the building so badly built that every sound from all the apartments could be heard clearly throughout the house. There was a drunken brawl in one apartment, I remember, and I was terrified. Finally, I got to the right door and at my knock a child opened a kitchen door. Inside, in a tiny hot room off the kitchen, was that mother lying in her bed almost wasted away to skin and bones. She told me that her sixteen-year-old boy had some work through the church and that was all the income the entire family of seven had. And I know of many other similar cases. In your life and work, Mrs. Harris, what have you found family life in a tenement means?

IH: It means misery to the entire family. You know, when the children go to school they are taught everything that's fine in life. And once a child starts to realize the good from the bad, and then has to go home to the bad, that child is ashamed of her own home and her surroundings.

ER: I know that, for I have heard the same thing from many others. But in the evenings, for instance, what do you do?

IH: There isn't anything at all to do. In the wintertime we all live in one room. There's no central heating and you have to heat up the house by making a coal stove. There isn't any privacy at all. If you want to take a bath in privacy, either you don't take it or you put the children out in the hall. If you are sick, you cannot be by yourself or keep warm and comfortable. The only toilets are the public ones in the halls and you catch more cold in going to one of them. My first child died because of those conditions. It got pneumonia and I had to take it outside and it caught cold on top of it. That's true.

ER: You have other children though, don't you, Mrs. Harris?

IH: Yes, two. My boy is twenty-one going on twenty-two. And my girl is nineteen.

ER: What do the young people do in these homes?

IH: They're only in it as little as they have to be, that's all. They try to go away where they can get a little comfort, something nice. Most of the boys go to the poolrooms. And some of the girls go places where they shouldn't go.

ER: I remember one of the most pathetic stories I ever heard was told by a man who came down to Washington. He had lived in an inside tenement, and one day, when he was at school with one of his children, his building caught fire. And when he got back his wife and four other children were burned to death.

IH: I know that man. One of those children went to school with my girl. We have her picture at home. I had the same experience myself, only thank God my children weren't burned to death.

ER: It seems to me that a city and its citizens who allow buildings of this kind to exist in it are partially responsible for deaths of this sort. As you doubtless know, Mrs. Harris, more than fifty low-rent housing projects have been built by the government in New York and in other cities during the Depression. First Houses on lower Broadway, the Williamsburg Project, another in the Bronx. Have you seen any of these new housing developments in New York?

IH: Yes, I went down to the First Houses when they were open. Once in a while I take a walk over to the Williamsburg Project and no matter when you come around, you find groups of people standing around, admiring, and you can see everyone is wishing they could get into them.

ER: I visited First Houses while they were being built and after families had moved into them. Each apartment there has a kitchen, a living room, and bathroom, and one, two, or three bedrooms according to the size of the place. And there are so many things to make life easier. I remember in the basements there are rooms for baby carriages so the mothers don't have to lug them upstairs.

IH: We have to lug them upstairs in our house or leave them downstairs to be broken or stolen.

ER: And then there are playrooms where children can play on rainy days, as well as playgrounds with trees and flowers and benches where mothers can sit and watch their children.

IH: Oh, that must be lovely. Our children can just play in the streets and they get hurt so often.

ER: The rooms are light and have air. There are windows in all the sleeping rooms.

IH: And closets. In our places you have to hang your clothes on the door or on the walls.

ER: And they are trying to keep the rent on those places within the range of the people who are now living in the tenements. I understand that the applications for the Williamsburg Project went out yesterday to 15,000 families. The rent on those apartments will range from around $4.50 to $7 per room per month.

IH: I hope I can get in the Williamsburg Houses. I know some people who are living in places like it now. They can't stop talking about how lovely the rooms are and the comfort they have. But Mrs. Roosevelt, I know you are very much interested in housing and you travel around the country a great deal seeing the conditions of other places outside New York. How do you find them?

ER: Well now, Mrs. Harris, before we talk about the places outside New York, Virginia Barr has a word to say.

(MIDDLE COMMERCIAL)

ER: In traveling throughout the country, I have visited families and homes of all kinds.

IH: Are some of those places as bad as what we people in New York have?

ER: People in other cities, both large and small, are up against exactly the same conditions you are. Not always as bad, but sometimes worse. Even in the country there are rural slums. I know of a place which might be called a shantytown right outside the city of Washington, where conditions are appalling. No sewage disposal, no running water, no streets. It's a wilderness right at the edge of a city, yet with none of the space available in a real wilderness. But on the other hand, some of the government homesteads show what suburban life may be. Greenbelt [Maryland], which is not yet open, about a half hour out of Washington, is designed as a low-rent housing project. There, anyone can live in all the comforts and decency any American family should have. Then at Reedsville [West Virginia], the Arthurdale Project is one where people have single houses and land to farm. I know where the people came from who live there now, and I know what it means to them.

IH: I guess we women are more interested in housing than the men are. Perhaps a man doesn't notice all the bad things. But we are in the house all day. We see everything that is wrong. What can we do to get better homes?

ER: The way we are going to do it is by awakening the public conscience to a realization of what bad housing means, not only to those who live in tenements but to the community as a whole. I think slums are a liability and no city should countenance them. It costs too much to have them. It would be much cheaper to have places where people could live in safety. Fires would not be such a menace. The city would not have to pay such big doctors' and hospital bills for people who contract serious illnesses in the slums. The police department would not have such a list of criminals. Children could be brought up to know other diversions than playing gangster in the streets. Once everyone understands this, there will not be the trouble in finding a way by which governments can help eliminate these conditions.

IH: I hope we don't have to wait very long, because we've been waiting for quite a long time.

ER: Do you think the kind of a home a man has can have an effect on his work?

IH: Of course. If he can walk into a pleasant home he feels as though he really wants to go on living and working for his family. But when he walks into a dirty, smelly hovel, it seems hopeless, that's all.

ER: I think that is another important point that should be taken into consideration by everyone who thinks about housing. Those who plan cities should plan industries and housing together. A worker's occupation and his home should not be too far apart. And his home should be healthful, so that illness does not take him off the job. It should be clean and neat, so he can reflect that cleanliness and be efficient and smart on the job. It should be a place where he can enjoy life, so that he can go out from it each day feeling that he wants to work to keep it, and his family happy. I think many men would find their way to better jobs and better pay, and the country as a whole would have better workers, if the homes in which the workers live encourage their ambitions and hope instead of killing them. Mrs. Harris, if you could have a nice little home, would you like it in the country?

IH: Oh, no. I don't want to leave the East Side. It's home. I don't think people should be made to move away from what they know. I like East Broadway. I would just like to have better houses down there.

ER: I can understand that perfectly. You told me that you would like to take all people who are against better housing to go on an inspection tour so that they could see what life in a tenement is like. I think you have shown us all a good deal tonight, and I hope that the few new developments we have talked about will help people realize what improvements are needed, and how necessary they are. (PAUSE)

And now Mrs. Harris and I must leave you. Mrs. Harris to return to New York, and I back to the White House to be present at a dinner for the Belgian premier. Next Wednesday evening, I shall be in Wilmington, Delaware, at my son's wedding. But I shall be with you, too, to tell you about White House plans for summer vacations, some of the things we are planning to do, and a few ideas that might interest you. Good night.

# 17.

# "Eleanor Roosevelt Interviewed on the Causes and Cures of War"

## RCA's The Magic Key Program

Sunday, January 9, 1938, 2:00–3:00 p.m. (NBC Blue Network)

*The Magic Key of RCA* was a Saturday night NBC Blue variety program that featured top stars such as Rudy Vallee, Irving Berlin, Fred Mac-Murray, Tommy Dorsey, and Eleanor Roosevelt. The program featured celebrity interviews, comedy sketches, and popular music.

Historian Allida Black observes that as war with Germany seemed increasingly likely, ER "struggled to reconcile her own anti-war sympathies with the information FDR presented on German conduct."[1] ER had condemned the Japanese invasion of China in her "My Day" column, and had praised the Abraham Lincoln Brigade fighting Fascists in Spain.

ER had recently published a short book, *This Troubled World*, in which she argued for economic boycotts and international cooperation to fend off war. But she also said military force may be necessary to deal with aggressors. In the *Magic Key* broadcast, ER describes the need for an international police force, foretelling the kind of world organization she would later help establish, the United Nations.

ANNOUNCER BEN GRAUER: In radio and television, it's RCA all the way!

(ORCHESTRA: "MAGIC KEY THEME")

ANNOUNCER MILTON CROSS: The Radio Corporation of America presents: *The Magic Key!*

(THEME SWELLS AND FINISHES)

CROSS: The Magic Key turns. One hundred and three leading radio stations from coast to coast in the United States, in Canada, Cuba, and Hawaii, are linked in one network to bring you this program in the interest of the family of RCA, whose members include RCA Victor, RCA Institutes, Radiomarine, RCA Communications, and the National Broadcasting Company. Today, the Radio Corporation of America presents Mrs. Franklin D. Roosevelt, speaking from Washington in a two-way interview with Linton Wells, in New York; the sensational new tenor of the Metropolitan Opera, Carl Hartmann; the popular rhythm stylist Joan Edwards; and Frank Black, who opens the program conducting the Magic Key Orchestra in the Andalusian dance "Ritmo," by Manuel Infante.

(ORCHESTRA)

(APPLAUSE)

(ORCHESTRA and VOCALIST)

CROSS: Living in the White House at Washington is an American wife, mother, and grandmother whose life is bound by special ties to the very fabric of our country's welfare. Today, international amity seems more difficult of achievement than ever before. But this discouraging outlook has served only to inspire this distinguished woman, Mrs. Franklin D. Roosevelt, to express her sincere beliefs on the subject of world peace. The family of RCA is honored to present the eminent author of a thoughtfully written new book, *This Troubled World*. Speaking from Washington, Mrs. Franklin D. Roosevelt will discuss the question of permanent world peace with Linton Wells, Magic Key commentator, in New York. The Magic Key turns to Linton Wells.

LW: Good afternoon, Mrs. Roosevelt.

ER: Good afternoon, Mr. Wells.

LW: Mrs. Roosevelt, being realists, we know that suspicions and hatreds among nations have brought this world of ours to the verge of chaos. Now, as never before, rational men and women search desperately for ways to reestablish international concord and advance the cause of peace on earth and goodwill toward men. America is acknowledged to be the world's most peace-loving nation. Yet we seem unable to inspire other countries to peaceful pursuits. Why do you think this has happened?

ER: The answer is simple. The causes of war are varied. Sometimes nations find themselves in restricted areas with growing populations. They must expand. This means conquering their neighbors and obtaining new territory, if not actually nearby, at least some territorial possessions in a more distant land. Or, nations lack raw materials. They are unable to produce certain necessary articles and this drives them to war in order to control the sources of materials which they consider necessary to their existence. Hereditary fear of other nations will force nations into a belligerent attitude, keep them constantly looking for trouble. This is good preparation for war but certainly no way to ensure peace.

In addition, internal conditions in nations can grow so bad that the people themselves will feel that life is so little worth living they might just as well go to war on the chance that they may improve their situation if they live through the war.

LW: History most certainly is filled with shocking examples of such international conduct.

ER: We are, fortunately, situated with enough land for our needs at present and an amazing amount of natural resources. We need comparatively little from other nations. We have few traditional fears. We are a self-confident and self-reliant people, and on the whole self-sufficient. Our fortunate situation, however, does not mean that we can persuade others to have the same sense of security that we have ourselves. And a sense of security is vital to a peaceful world. That is why we haven't been successful in making other nations adopt our own attitude. Their circumstances are different; they cannot very well see our point of view.

LW: Mrs. Roosevelt, you have said that it is easier to keep out of situations which lead to war than it is to bring about peace once war is going on. We also understand that you have been asked to consider idealistic permanent peace plans without number. Undoubtedly you must have evolved a plan of your own which would safeguard the peace of the world, if it could be sincerely tried out. Won't you please tell us about it?

ER: In writing my book, *This Troubled World*, I stated that I thought there was no plan which could, at the present time, ensure peace. For we must have a real change in human nature as a basis for any permanent peace plan. I think, however, that we should work toward the getting together of representatives of different nations, either in sectional groups or in a central group. Gradually, nations will come to feel that they can bring their grievances and problems to these groups for discussion. In that way they can get world opinion to help them solve their difficulties before they actually come to using force.

LW: Granted that the present League of Nations has failed to maintain world peace, why do you think a reconstituted international body with a strong police force would be any more successful?

ER: The present League of Nations does not represent every nation in the world. And whether we like to acknowledge it or not, the fact that we are not in it has militated against its success. We are a strong and peace-loving nation, and can, because of our position, hold to an objective and disinterested point of view. An international body which was truly representative, and which devoted itself to research and discussion, would be very helpful in preventing wars. It would have to be backed, however, by peoples who truly wanted peace and tried to exercise the kind of self-discipline and self-restraint and unselfishness which the maintenance of peace requires. A police force will be essential, I think, for a time, just as it is essential in communities to enable us to restrain the elements which insist on the use of force in opposition to the will of the majority of nations.

LW: Admittedly, the preservation of our civilization seems to demand a change in the attitude of humans toward each other. But this means changing human nature, and how do you think that can be done?

ER: By education and by spiritual growth. Admittedly, if all of us lived according to the doctrines of Christ, many of our internal problems would solve themselves. As well as external problems. But we are not accustomed to regarding questions that come up from the point of view of the Nazarene. It will take time to educate people to the realization that this point of view is an eminently practical one, which we were meant to live by.

LW: Do you really believe, Mrs. Roosevelt, that people can be taught the meaning of brotherly love and be persuaded to practice it?

ER: Why, of course I do. Certainly.

LW: We of the older generation know that there is no such thing as glory in war. But how can we strip war of its aura of heroic fiction and convince the adventurous youth of our country that, at best, it is a ghastly, useless struggle of destruction and extermination?

ER: Again, by education. And by an effort on the part of our generation to keep before youth a real picture of war, and the futility of the belief that wars have really settled the questions over which they were fought.

LW: One final question, Mrs. Roosevelt. Is it your belief that the

United States could restore stability to the world by maintaining its land, sea, and air forces on a basis of second-to-none on Earth?

ER: Certainly not. No one nation can be arrogant enough to believe that if they build up a tremendous war machine they will not have the same temptation to use it as other nations have in the past. We, like other nations, must have adequate forces for defense. Of course, this does not mean that any one nation, by itself, can achieve world peace by being the world's policeman. This can only be achieved by an honest desire on the part of all the nations concerned, and by mutual cooperation.

LW: Thank you very much, Mrs. Roosevelt, for the encouragement you have given us today. We sincerely hope that what you have said and written will aid materially in solving the problems of this troubled world. Good-bye, Mrs. Roosevelt.

ER: Good-bye, Mr. Wells.

GRAUER: You have just heard Mrs. Franklin D. Roosevelt speaking from Washington in a two-way interview with Linton Wells in New York, on the subject of world peace, as discussed in her recently published book, *This Troubled World*. This is the National Broadcasting Company.

# 18.

# "Domestic Workers and Government Housing"

*Mrs. Eleanor Roosevelt's Own Program,*
presented by SweetHeart Soap

Tuesday, May 21, 1940, 1:15–1:30 p.m. (NBC Red Network)

In 1940, Americans from all corners of the country sent the White House letters and postcards variously demanding or pleading with FDR to keep the United States out of war. In October 1940, FDR repeated his pledge that America's war buildup was for defensive preparation only, that American boys would not be sent to any foreign wars.

Until 1938, FDR held out hope that the crisis in Europe might be settled through negotiation rather than war. He was loath to lead Americans where they did not want to go, which was a military clash overseas. After World War I, many Americans believed they had been forced into a conflict that was none of their business. Anti-interventionist sentiment was strong in 1940, and one of the nation's great heroes, aviator Charles Lindbergh, was a leading spokesman for the cause.

But when Adolf Hitler annexed Austria and seized the Czechoslovak Sudetenland, it was clear to FDR that appeasement would fail. The problem was how to convince the nation that it should start preparing for war. Historian Lynne Olson demonstrates that FDR made no effort in the 1930s to convince Americans that they should help stop the Fascist dictators. "The increasingly dire events in Europe only confirmed their determination to stay as far away from that hornet's nest as possible," Olson writes.[1] The administration maintained an official policy of neutrality, and FDR was up for reelection in 1940.

ER's deep commitment to peace was also challenged by the events in Europe and Asia. As war approached, she was expected to support the administration's war-preparation efforts. She openly endorsed FDR's armaments program in 1938. She supported proposed changes to the Neutrality Act in 1939 to allow weapons sales to France and England. *Time* quoted ER saying, "I see no reason for us entering the war—as yet."[2] She told a reporter for *Harper's* that if the United States stayed out of the war while France and Britain fought the battle for freedom, "we should be living for ourselves alone."[3]

When listeners wrote to ask what she thought about planning for war, ER answered them on the radio and in her newspaper column. Democracy relied on an engaged and tolerant citizenry, she said. The kind of prejudices fueling Nazi ideology had no place in the United States, she argued, and would only serve to weaken the country. She insisted that a healthy democracy also demanded free expression of ideas and political opposition, even from the government's most virulent critics.

In the fall of 1940, ER began a new series of commercial broadcasts on Tuesday and Thursday afternoons against a backdrop of fast-moving calamities in Europe. Germany had invaded France. Some 300,000 British and French troops had barely avoided getting wiped out at the French port of Dunkirk. Paris would soon fall to the Nazis and the

German Luftwaffe would begin a furious bombing campaign against British cities.

The thirteen-week series of national programs was sponsored by SweetHeart Soap. ER was paid $3,000 per program and announced that the proceeds would, again, go to the American Friends Service Committee. By this time, she was paying tax on the earnings first. *Mrs. Roosevelt's Own Program* was a mix of subjects thought to appeal to women—dining at the White House, the joys of picnicking—with more serious subjects like the problem of European war orphans, women and national defense, and life inside a national political campaign. After each broadcast, scores of listeners wrote to ER as they always did. Some sent their letters to the SweetHeart Soap Company in New York, which typed up a weekly digest of their comments and concerns. Others wrote to the radio station, the network, or simply addressed their envelopes to ER at the White House or Hyde Park, New York. ER answered many of the letters but did not respond to the most vicious. These included a woman describing herself as an American mother of two sons, who wrote:

I have just listened to your combination of politics and soap peddling over the NBC. It seems to me you could do a lot more for yourself and the nation if you would stay home and try to persuade your foolish husband to keep his nose out of European embroilment.[4]

A typewritten postcard from San Francisco read:

Why don't you use some of this soap to scrub those BUCK TEETH of yours and maybe you could talk plainer . . . Why don't you go jump in the bay and let the young people get some work, when we all know that the old cripple is worth millions.[5]

Either ER or her secretary, Malvina Thompson, had marked these letters "N.A." for no answer. But they were still kept on file.

ANNOUNCER: This is *Mrs. Eleanor Roosevelt's Own Program*, presented by SweetHeart Soap!

(MUSIC "UP AND OUT")

ANNOUNCER: And again, we greet Mrs. Eleanor Roosevelt! Today Mrs. Roosevelt takes time out from her countless other interests to chat with us from the nation's capital. These intimate talks come to you with the compliments of SweetHeart Soap, one of America's favorite beauty soaps for the past half-century. And now, we won't keep you waiting a minute longer. Are you ready, Washington, DC? Then please come in, Mrs. Eleanor Roosevelt!

ER: There is one thing about every woman's home which I think has never been sufficiently emphasized. Namely, that household work is a profession. If you do the household work yourself, you will find it most satisfying and you will be able to do more for your husband and children and to include more outside interests in your life if you learn to schedule your time. If you have a routine for everything you do, you will be astonished to find how much you can increase your speed. In dealing with little children, of course, it is impossible to hurry them. And one has to realize that, in order to allow them to learn to do things for themselves, one is obliged to take a great deal more time in letting them struggle over things which could easily be done for them. In the long run, however, this too saves time. And teaching a child a routine is one of the best lessons which can be learned in the home.

In many households throughout the country, one or more people are employed for household work. This is one of the fields which is not oversupplied and many people have come to look upon this as a possible new profession. Two elements enter into the successful development, however, of this field of employment. One is the proper training of the household employee. The other is the proper training which the homemaker must have as an employer of labor. The approach to the whole situation has been a bad one in the past. There were no regular hours and the living conditions and working conditions were peculiarly unsatisfactory. That was because the majority of women did not approach the running of a house as a man would approach the running of his business. If one person was taken on to work in the home, the woman of the home was apt to think that the [housekeeper] would do all the work which was to be done without any regard to standards in hours and wages. No man employs an assistant in his business and expects the assistant to take over the whole running of the business. No woman employing one or more people in her home can ever expect to run it satisfactorily unless she schedules the time of her employees and has a complete understanding as to what each person in her household is expected to do, [and] sees to it that the living and working conditions are good and takes a personal interest in those who work with her. This makes the home a good place in which to live.

In the last few years, largely through the interest of the Young Women's Christian Association and a few different groups of women, great strides have been made in interesting women to set up standards for household employees. I believe if we educate the employer, we will soon find a much more satisfactory situation, which will mean employment for many women on a more or less professional basis. There are women being trained today to go into homes on an eight-hour-a-day schedule. There are women being trained as specialists for certain specific work in the home, such as the care of children, or cooking, or laundry work, or waitresses, or housemaids. But the vast majority of workers will be wanted as general houseworkers, doing a little of everything.

In certain parts of the country, the household employees will be in the majority, colored. But that does not mean that, of necessity, they must be less well trained or receive lower wages. If the work is worth doing, it is worth doing well and it should receive adequate compensation. Where board and room are given which is of a satisfactory nature, that should be taken into consideration in the agreement on wages. But the important thing is a clear understanding before the worker takes the position. We have states today which have recognized household employment as a profession and have passed laws which govern such employment. As yet there is no organization in this field. And I imagine because of the close individual association between people, it will be difficult for a union to form very definite rules governing this type of organization. Therefore, it is important that there should be education on both sides, a sense of mutual responsibility, and a recognition of the fact that the relationship of individuals in the home has a great deal to do with the atmosphere which exists in that home.

But before we continue, I believe New York has a message for us. Let's listen.

ANNOUNCER: Many thanks, and I'll only take a minute, Mrs. Roosevelt. Friends, it's exactly three weeks ago that Mrs. Roosevelt began this series of broadcasts—a series which has already won a well-deserved place on America's "must listen" list. And already the letters are pouring in—letters from folks who'd been on the verge of trying the product responsible for these programs, SweetHeart Soap. Thousands of these people are now actually using SweetHeart Soap, and folks, you just ought to hear their comments. At last, they say, we've found a bath and beauty soap that's so pure and gentle, so wonderfully thorough, so delightfully mild and fragrant that every bath and cleanup is a real joy. And the grandest part of it is the way the whole family enjoys pure, delicately fragrant SweetHeart Soap. Well, all I want to add is this: SweetHeart Soap is yours for only a few pennies a cake, very likely less than you're spending now. So try it real soon. Why not today? Remember the name: SweetHeart Soap. And now we take you back to Washington, DC, and our welcome speaker, Mrs. Eleanor Roosevelt.

ER: Now, for a moment, I want to talk to you about the general question of housing. It seems to me that every woman in this country must be deeply concerned with this problem. That is one industry—building—which means a great deal in the way of general employment. The building of houses brings about much employment in allied fields. This country needs about 900,000 new homes a year for at least a decade. Of these, one-third should be for the top-income third; one-third should be for the middle-income third, and in both of these brackets, private capital can find an outlet and make money. The last one-third should be for the lowest-income group. Here is where the government has come into the field. Private industry has not built at all for this group, and so the United States Housing Authority was organized. This authority is now providing about 60,000 homes a year. These homes rent anywhere from $7.00 a month in certain places in the South to $17.00 a month in New York City.

These homes are restricted to the people with annual incomes ranging from about $550 to $1,050 a year. It has been found necessary to do this so that there should be no competition with private industry. Approximately 360,000 homes a year are built by private industry for the highest-income group. Sixty thousand a year are built for the middle-income group. Even the low-cost housing, subsidized in large part by the government, helps business, because the materials going into these homes have to be bought in the open market and the production of these materials provides employment. It has been the experience in both England and Wales that this type of building encouraged building by private industry.

Ever since the United States Housing Authority has been at work, we have been gradually clearing our slums, both in urban and rural areas. This is a relief to the taxpayers, for slum areas are extremely expensive for the community. Out of them come our greatest number of criminals and public charges in hospitals and insane asylums. They cost us more in police protection and fire protection than any other part of our communities and yet we forget to add all these things in when we compute the cost of the appropriations which are made for low-cost housing. It has always seemed to me that this program should make special appeal to the women, who know the value of home life and spend so much of their time in the creation of homes.

Before a jury of representative women in Washington the other day, I heard a New York City mother tell the story of her family. She lived in one of those old-type tenements that have windows in the front and back only, and the bedrooms in between have no ventilation. Out of her family of six, one child was in a tuberculosis sanitarium and all the others were in the outdoor classes in the New York City public school system, which meant that [other students] were threatened with tuberculosis. This condition is due in part to malnutrition, but much of it is due to bad housing.

We women realize what this means to the future of this country and we are the ones to urge doing something about it. If you live in a community where there are housing projects, you should go to see them and become interested in them and register your interest with your representatives of your state and federal government. Projects of this kind depend upon public opinion. As a woman you probably have a more vivid understanding than has any man of what decent homes mean to the community and what sanitary conditions mean, especially to the children. Next Thursday, I think I shall talk a little about gardens, which seem to me something one should think about even in a city.

(MUSIC)

ANNOUNCER: Thank you very much, Mrs. Roosevelt. Folks, we're proud of the fact that SweetHeart Soap has won over five million new users in the last two years. We think it's a fine tribute to this fifty-five-year-favorite soap. But some of you listeners haven't tried SweetHeart Soap as yet, and I want you to know why you should.

SweetHeart Soap is pure, and therefore mild. It agrees with your skin. SweetHeart Soap is thorough, so it removes stubborn surface impurities that might spoil natural skin charm. And SweetHeart lends you a lovely, delicate fragrance for extra pleasure in every bath and cleanup. Five million new users discovered all this just lately, so why not make pure, delicately fragrant SweetHeart Soap your personal discovery too? When you do we're confident that you'll join those delighted thousands who say, "There's no other soap like it!"

(MUSIC)

ANNOUNCER: And this brings us to the end of another visit with Mrs. Eleanor Roosevelt. Be sure to set your radio dials for this same station, same time, next Thursday, when Mrs. Roosevelt again comes to call on her friends all over America. Meantime, be sure to provide yourself with the fine product that presents these programs, SweetHeart Soap, famous for fifty years as the soap that agrees with your skin. Now it's good-bye until next Thursday, when you'll again hear . . .

(MUSIC "UP AND OUT")

ANNOUNCER: *Mrs. Eleanor Roosevelt's Own Program*! Ed Herlihy speaking.

# 19.

# "Questions About the White House"

*Mrs. Eleanor Roosevelt's Own Program,*
presented by SweetHeart Soap

Tuesday, June 4, 1940

ER: Good day, ladies and gentlemen. I have received a great many interesting letters since we started these radio talks. I want to thank you for
writing to me, and I would like to tell you how much I appreciate your
comments and specific suggestions. As I promised you before, I hope to
answer as many of your questions as possible. But because they are of
such a varied nature, it is necessary to group them and select a number
of related questions for each broadcast. So, if your question has not yet
been answered, I hope you will bear with me.

Your most frequent requests are for information about the White
House, how it runs, how the many tasks are divided, and a host of other
details. So today, I have invited Mrs. Genevieve Forbes Herrick to come
to the studio with me and, by acting as your spokesman, to help me
answer your many questions. Being interviewed by Mrs. Herrick is not a

novelty for me. For some time, Mrs. Herrick has been a regular member of the group of correspondents with whom I have regular press conferences in Washington. So I want you to meet Mrs. Herrick now.

GH: Thank you, Mrs. Roosevelt. It's indeed a pleasure to act as spokesman for your many radio friends. Having looked through some of their many letters, it seems that almost everyone is interested in the White House. And I suppose that is only natural because the White House is the symbolic home of the nation. Just how many people would you say visit the White House every year?

ER: Last year we had some 1,320,300 visitors. Of that number, 4,729 had meals—either lunch, dinner, or tea—23,267 came in groups to be received, and 264,060 were sightseers. And 323 were houseguests. You can see, Mrs. Herrick, that the White House is a sort of Mecca for patriotic pilgrims.

GH: And what would you say, Mrs. Roosevelt, is the one thing that most White House visitors want to see?

ER: I believe they are most anxious to see the portraits of George and Martha Washington in the East Room. But almost every individual or group has something about which they are most curious. This varies of course. Some want to see the new Lincoln portrait, others the White House china, and so on and on.

GH: Now, do the children who visit the White House have some particular favorite, Mrs. Roosevelt?

ER: I think of late the children like best the room where the president exhibits the collection of things which are sent to him personally. This exhibit, which is constantly changed, includes ship models and many other curios. Some of them are really beautiful.

GH: What about yourself, Mrs. Roosevelt? Is there some feature of the White House which you find most interesting?

ER: That is hard to decide, Mrs. Herrick, because the entire house is so fascinating. Perhaps it is the atmosphere of the second floor that

I like best. This part of the house seems somehow to be charged with the personalities of all the great people who have lived there in the past.

GH: I think I know what you mean. I've had the feeling, while visiting some historic places, that the greatness of past deeds and men still lingers. And while we're on the subject, which of the symbols of patriotism in Washington seems to you most representative of our American democracy?

ER: I think perhaps the Washington Monument is the one that most people would mention, because you see it from so many different places when you come to Washington. But the monument from which I get the most inspiration is the Lincoln Memorial. The statue of Lincoln is in itself so beautiful, and his words carved on the wall always deepen my belief in democracy.

GH: Well, it seems like a big jump from the Lincoln Memorial to the problems of housekeeping for the White House, but if I'm to be spokesman for your listeners, I must get back to their questions. Who does all the shopping and marketing for the White House, Mrs. Roosevelt?

ER: Well, Mrs. Herrick, in housekeeping for the White House, there's more than just shopping and marketing. You have to keep the accounts, and those are the most complicated kind of bookkeeping. Everything has to be kept in detail so that you know just what every meal costs per person and you know just where to charge it, because of course, as you know, there is a division between the personal expenses of the president and his family, and state expenses. These are the duties of Mrs. [Henrietta] Nesbitt, the housekeeper.

GH: Now, another of your radio friends wants to know who does all the laundry and the mending required for such a large house, with so many guests.

ER: Many of my own friends have asked me that same question. The White House laundry is done by two women in their own homes. They are regularly employed by the week. One woman takes all the flat wash and the other takes the body clothes. It is a very large wash, and the mending takes a great deal of time. All the housemaids in the White House work on putting the laundry away, and mending it in their spare time, after the work of looking after the rooms and guests is done. I see you have some more questions, Mrs. Herrick.

GH: Well, we've covered shopping, marketing, laundering, and mending. Now we have a question from a woman who wants to know if all the historic china, which visitors see in the White House, is actually used.

ER: No, not all of it. Much of the historic china, of which you see samples in the china room, has long been out of use because there is not much of it left, and the few remaining pieces are highly prized. There are certain times when some of these pieces are used. For instance, it has been the custom at state receptions to use the beautiful punch bowls which were bought during Mr. Lincoln's administration for lemonade and fruit punch. But for regular White House service, china of recent days is used. Certain portions of the older sets are used when there is enough for the number of guests. Some of the china bought in Mr. Theodore Roosevelt's administration, and some of the salad plates bought in Mr. Cleveland's administration, have been used on such occasions.

GH: That is most interesting to me, Mrs. Roosevelt, because it illustrates so vividly the great historic value of everything in the White House, even to the dishes. I believe it was Dolly Madison who once called Washington "the nation's drawing room." Thanks in part to you, that narrowly social definition has been greatly expanded. Won't you give us your definition of Washington today?

ER: Washington—or the District of Columbia, as I have been urged to call it—today really represents the center of governmental authority. There was a time when financial authority was more important than governmental authority, but today that is no longer so. One is conscious, in Washington, of being near the really supreme authority of the country.

GH: You just mentioned something that has changed in Washington. Isn't it true, Mrs. Roosevelt, that much remains unchanged? I have often heard people in Washington talk about precedence. Perhaps your radio friends would like to know just what precedence means, and how the problems of precedence at the White House are handled.

GH: I suppose I could refer you to the State Department, Mrs. Herrick, because they are the authority on all rules of precedence. But perhaps I can answer your question. Simply stated, the rules of precedence are traditions handed down which govern the procedure at state ceremonies. Precedence exists in Washington as it exists in no other part of the United States. It is important, first, because the people representing foreign governments are accustomed to a rule of precedence, either because of position or because of birth. Second, because official positions in Washington are also governed by certain rules of precedence.

The State Department handles all of these questions. They seat the people at state dinners, and they advise us just how we should deal with certain problems when important visitors come from other lands. This is a great help, and I have always been grateful that decisions in the very complicated matters of precedence did not lie with me.

GH: While you're discussing the subject of entertaining in the White House, I'm sure you can answer a question that everyone must wonder about. You meet so many people, Mrs. Roosevelt, shake so many hands, don't they all seem alike to you by the time an affair is almost over?

ER: No, indeed, Mrs. Herrick. I make it a point to look at every face, and it's astonishing how interesting the faces are. Of course, after I have shaken hands with several hundred people, I begin to get tired. Sometimes, people blur before my eyes and I can only hope that the smile on my face still expresses my pleasure in seeing them. I think the story which I have repeated many times rather expresses what many of my guests are thinking as they are received. One lady wrote to me, after

I had shaken hands with several hundred people: "Mrs. Roosevelt, do you shake and think, or do you just stand and shake?"

GH: Well, Mrs. Roosevelt, I've finished all the questions I can ask today, but I promise I won't shake hands. I'll just say good-bye and thank you so much for inviting me here today.

ER: You've been a great help, Mrs. Herrick. In fact, it was such a pleasure to have you that I wish you would return on Thursday and continue with the interview. Will you?

GH: Oh, gladly.

ANNOUNCER: Thank you very much, Mrs. Roosevelt and Mrs. Herrick.

# 20.

# "Democracy"

*Mrs. Eleanor Roosevelt's Own Program,*
presented by SweetHeart Soap

Thursday, June 20, 1940

ER: Good day, ladies and gentlemen. I have put off until now answering some of the serious questions which have come in because the times are so serious that I felt most of you had enough gloomy things to think about without concentrating on something serious on this program. I notice, however, that in our family, we discuss these serious problems around the table, and every member of the family is keenly interested in them. So today we will turn to some of these questions. Many letters have arrived asking me to talk about democracy, to tell how I think everyone in this land can have a satisfying life, how people can live and not die for democracy, how we can share the work, the joys, and the sorrows in this world so that we may all be able to enjoy life, liberty, and the pursuit of happiness.

Well, the first way, of course, is to really try to become a democratic center in the community, to be a person to whom people will turn with the knowledge that they will have a hearing. In this way, you will really know about your community and serve to interpret the meaning of democracy as a way of life.

A representative democracy such as ours is a government which allows its people to govern through the election of representatives. People here are free to express their convictions through the ballot and, if they exercise their power intelligently, they choose good leaders who really represent them. But self-government does not end with the ballot. It is your duty to follow up with the people you elect to see that they perform their duties. Politically, this is what one should do in a democracy where citizens take their duties seriously.

When an entire community has a sense of responsibility for everyone in it, as well as for the community as a whole, then democracy is more than a word—it is a way of life. Under this democratic way of life, every citizen is assured certain things, namely the right to an adequate return for one's labor in whatever field one is able to contribute it; the right to obtain an education as far as one's ability allows one to pursue it; the right to basic freedoms of the press, of assembly, of speech, and of religion. And to these rights we must add a concern that every individual shall have a decent place in which to live, a decent chance for health, and adequate recreation. Under those circumstances, democracy lives, grows, and has meaning for every citizen.

In a democratic community it is not necessary that everyone shall have the same things, for all people's desires and aspirations are not the same. But under such a government everyone shall have equal opportunity, and it is opportunity which is the lifeblood of democracy. It may be necessary for us to die as well as to live for democracy, but we will die gladly to protect this type of freedom and justice for every individual. Dying will seem preferable to living under certain restraints.

In times such as this, it is necessary for every one of us to reexamine some of the fundamental concepts of democracy. We must redefine such words as "patriotism." We must be sure to understand what the American flag stands for. The American flag represents our history and our ideals. We came from thirteen original states and we have grown from these little red and white bars to the forty-eight symbolized by our forty-eight stars. Patriotism is something which makes me think—as I look at an American flag—of the things I love: the country whose soil is dear to me. I think of the ideals for which other Americans have sacrificed themselves.

Not so long ago, I received a letter which included the interesting thought that some Americans who traced their ancestry to the *Mayflower* took their freedom for granted. The same writer also points out that many other Americans who have come here more recently sometimes abuse our American freedom. I suppose this is a reference to the groups amongst us that are banded together as Nazis, Fascists, or Communists. These groups are troublesome largely because we do not know how great is their influence. Since we have neglected, in many cases, to translate democracy into a way of life for all the people in the nation, and we fear, therefore, the effect of the promise of better things even when those promises are not backed up by performance.

Another correspondent asks what the ordinary woman with limited time and talents can do to become a better citizen. The question of better citizenship for men and women is tied up today, in their minds, with the world situation. Almost every woman I know is marking time until she can really feel that the government has called upon her to do some specific job into which she can throw all her energies. Perhaps the first thing to do, however, is to see to it that we remain calm, poised, and continue to do the things which are routine daily tasks. For instance, I think it is important today that a child returning from school should find a poised, calm mother to whom to bring joys and sorrows, and not one who is jittery and frightened and who takes him convulsively in her arms and talks to him of the dangers which lurk on every side.

I think it is vitally important that we face the present world situation with reality, and consider all the possibilities and probabilities of our future. These have been put before us and will be put before us more and more clearly by the president and responsible people in the government. We owe it not only to ourselves but to the world to preserve our democracy and its freedoms, and we can do it by thinking our problems through calmly and sanely. We cannot do it if we become hysterical and frightened. We probably have a Fifth Column in this country and we do not know where it is or who it is. But we cannot all appoint ourselves unofficial agents to persecute people whom we suspect. There is a properly constituted branch of the government—the Department of Justice—to which any citizen, or alien for that matter, can report anxieties and to which they can apply for protection, which our laws have assured us.

We must do all we can to prevent the rise of racial or religious hatred in this country. And I feel that much of this calm assurance of spirit must come from the women. It is obvious to me that this is a long-time job and it will require the cooperation of men, women, and young people all over this country. It may seem to you that a racial or religious prejudice which does not touch you is something about which you need not concern yourself. But unfortunately, these prejudices do not stay within the bounds of any one category. The feeling spreads and one prejudice engenders another, and a people soon find themselves a prey to fears of all kinds.

This means that we must not believe all the rumors which are spread, and that we should make every effort to find out the truth before we allow ourselves to become too greatly concerned. I have heard many fantastic stories about myself and my family and have never been able to discover their beginnings. I am sure that nearly everyone else has had the same experience. It is far more important to weigh everything you read and hear today in order not to be a party to any injustice or unfairness. The history of what has happened in some countries in Europe should be a terrible example to us. We have proved that we can live in this country in peace with many different racial and religious groups, and we must keep that before us if we hope to prove to the world that the democratic way of life is far superior to any other.

No matter how limited your time or talents, you can give what you have to give to your country by knowing your own community and advocating such laws as will help to make democracy worthwhile for every individual. The diligent living of your citizenship, from day to day, may mean success for democracy in the world of the future, or absolute failure for our ideals.

# 21.

# "Political Conventions and Campaign Trips"

*Mrs. Eleanor Roosevelt's Own Program,*
presented by SweetHeart Soap

Tuesday, June 25, 1940

ER: Good day, ladies and gentlemen. This is the time for conventions. And of course the ones which will draw the greatest attention are those of the two major political parties. The Republican Convention is already meeting in Philadelphia. The Democrats meet in convention next month in Chicago. We are a politically minded country and we enjoy our political struggles and our differences of opinion in a way which I think probably few other countries really understand.

When the conventions are over, the two party leaders usually take a little time off for rest before the real campaign begins. This year, of course, we have had a number of Republican candidates for the nomination for the presidency, traveling around the country allowing the people an opportunity to see and hear them. This is never necessary for men who are well known nationally, but it must be done when one is trying to break into the national political picture.

When once the nominations are made and the campaigns begin, the candidates plan not only radio broadcasts for themselves and the usual campaign setup for everyone else, but they start off on speaking trips throughout the country. I should like to describe to you, in general terms, one of these campaign trips which might be taken by a Republican or a Democratic candidate. I am talking to you from the point of view of one who has been many miles on campaign trains, always as an onlooker. This has given me an opportunity to be a bit objective, and while I realize the seriousness underlying the purpose of these trips, I have still been able to enjoy some of the humorous superficialities.

The point of departure is usually someplace where a group of people gather to bid the party candidate Godspeed. Almost always the candidate has some friends and members of his family in the party. Of course, the candidate is the only person who is legally up for election. But the public seems to take an interest in his entire family, and sometimes one has the feeling that the public considers the whole family responsible to *them* for their actions from the time of the nomination on.

There is a large group of newspaper reporters on the train—and today there are women reporters as well as men—photographers and even newsreel men. Someone is put in charge of these press representatives, and his job is to get them in touch with the candidate when necessary, and to get the advance copies of speeches, et cetera, and to help them to get their stories sent from the train at stated intervals. There is usually an office staff because work goes on all during the campaign trip.

If a president is running for reelection, he is, of course, surrounded by Secret Service men during his campaign trip. If he is merely a candidate for the first time, he is unprotected except for the local police until he is elected to office. This is a great change, and one of the things to which it is very hard for most men to accustom themselves. The law requires that the president of the United States be protected by the Secret Service. And whether he likes it or not, he must be amenable to the rules which they lay down for his protection. He has spent many years of his life unguarded except by his own right arm, and most of the time he hasn't felt that he was in any particular danger on account of the malevolence of other people. But the day he becomes president he is a target for all the prejudices and grievances which may arise among 120 million people. Well-balanced people express their grievances through the regular political channels. But the totally unbalanced—and there are some of these in every large nation—also may try to express their political ideas. These unfortunate people have no real idea of why they feel as they do and they are not responsible for their actions. It is against such people that the state must constantly protect the chief executive.

At times it must be most irritating to feel that there is an ever-present possibility of physical danger. But after a while I imagine that a man learns to ignore his ever-present bodyguards. In a sense, we all make this kind of adjustment. For example, we hardly realize that everywhere we go there are police who look after our safety. And we are not conscious of their eternal vigilance until their protection is needed. But a political candidate must be willing and able to make any adjustments. He must be big enough to step in and fill a position which is surrounded with restrictions, accompanied by a certain amount of pomp and ceremony. Then he must also be able to make the adjustment of stepping out of that picture and again living as plain Mr. American Citizen. I am sure that some presidents must have felt the greatest relief in the world on leaving their office and resuming normal private life. To others, it must be a fairly difficult adjustment to change from the nation's number-one citizen to one of the nation's 120 million citizens.

But I have gone a little astray in this discussion. Before a [campaign train] trip is started, regular stops are arranged. Some places will be selected for long station stops where the candidate will leave the train to make a major speech. The man who is in charge of the train schedule has a most trying assignment. While a campaign trip is in progress, he is constantly bombarded with telegrams from small cities, towns, and villages along the route, asking that the train stop there for just a minute so the people from the country 'round about can catch a glimpse of the candidate.

In the course of a day, a train may make two or three major stops where the candidate makes a real speech. But there may be ten or twelve one-to-three-minute stops where only a few words are spoken. The candidate's family is always asked to be on the back platform for these short stops. The local politicians are always present and each of them say a few words, if that can possibly be arranged. Flowers are brought to the ladies of the party and sometimes other gifts, and crowds gather around the observation platform in the rear of the train. There is always a tense moment before the train starts again for fear some child is on the roof or near the wheels, for the crowds clamber about everywhere and the children sometimes choose dangerous places from which to view the proceedings. I remember in one place seeing some small boys being hauled off the roof of the president's car by the Secret Service, and I have often heard them urge youngsters to keep away from the wheels. In all the trips I have taken, I never remember a real accident, but I have had many anxious moments.

We also have had some amusing instances. On one campaign trip, when I was not on board, my daughter regaled me with detail about one of the newspaperwomen missing the train because she was caught in the crowd and could not get back. Without knowing she was not on board, the signal was given to start the train and the poor woman had to take a taxicab and chase the train! Fortunately, there were so many stops to make that she caught up, but a good many miles away. I've seen photographers clambering on to the back platform as the train was slowly pulling out.

When these stops are over and the train is on its way again, all of us go back to whatever we had been doing—playing cards, reading, sewing, working, or whatever it may be. The candidate talks to the local politicians who get on the train and ride for a short distance, or prepares his next speech. Sometimes, if the family is honest with the candidate, they will tease him a little about the similarity of his speeches. But they must be tolerant with him because I am sure there is just as little pleasure in repeating the same speech over and over again as there is in hearing it.

It seems as though one has hardly settled down after a stop when someone comes along calling: "All out on the back platform for another stop," and everything has to be dropped. Occasionally these stops will come during mealtime and everyone dashes out holding a napkin in one hand and wondering if the food will be too cold to eat when they get back. But the entire campaign party must be at the beck and call of the crowds, night and day, all during the trip. People may clamber about the campaign train even after everyone aboard has gone to bed. If the candidate is very young and very anxious to please, he will get out of bed, put on a wrapper, and respond to the call of his public.

The only thing about campaign trips which has always seemed to me rather futile is that the greater part of those who come to see a candidate and listen to him are people who agree with him and probably would vote for him in any case. Of course, there are exceptions. There must be a number of people who are really swayed by personal contact with the candidate.

I do not suppose that we will ever get away from campaign trips. And I think, perhaps, we would miss them. For there is something in the American people which makes them want to get a face-to-face impression of the other fellow. Campaign trips undoubtedly have a great deal of value for the candidate, too. He gets a panoramic impression of his fellow American citizens and of the country as a whole. He gets a clear idea of the vastness of our nation, of the great mixture of peoples and views. In other words, while the candidate is barnstorming to let the voters get a look at him, he is giving himself an excellent opportunity to get a look at the voters. So here's to all those who are going out to court the vote of their fellow citizens, and may whatever is best for the country come to pass on Election Day!

# 22.

# "Planning for War and Postwar Periods"

*Mrs. Eleanor Roosevelt's Own Program,*
presented by SweetHeart Soap

Thursday, June 27, 1940

ER: Good day, ladies and gentlemen. In the many years that I have been interested in and connected with public affairs, I cannot remember a single time when people wanted more ardently to be of service to their country. Men, women, and even children are anxious to serve in any way they can, and yet there seems to be no very evident way in which their energies may be harnessed. The result is that the more energetic citizens are thinking up plans of their own and trying, in every way, to get people to adopt their ideas. This, unfortunately, may have some rather curious and haphazard effects. All of us must understand that in a country as large as ours, effort must be organized, plans must be worked out carefully in a unified program, people's activities and resources must be coordinated either under the government or under a few well-organized private agencies, working in cooperation with each other and with the government.

In the meantime, it seems to me that the obvious course of action for most of us is to go on with our jobs, whatever they may be. If possible, we should try to do our selected tasks a little better than before. Wherever it lies in our power, we should try to give work to somebody else. A man or a woman who is unemployed, a girl or a boy without a job, can never be happy because they feel that they are a drag upon the country rather than an asset. We must recognize that there is something wrong with an economy which does not supply every able-bodied citizen who is willing to work some gainful employment at a living wage. Since our economy is out of joint, the government must step in until we get it going again.

The nationwide spontaneous desire to be of service to the country is nothing more than the will of a democracy to preserve itself. It is true that the first step in preserving democracy is to see that every single citizen has an opportunity to earn a livelihood. A second and equally important step is to build up in each of us a sense of responsibility for all the others. During the past weeks, I have been flooded with letters from people in every part of the country suggesting ways in which we can increase our usefulness. Some of them are excellent, some impractical, and some amusing. For example, one writer sponsors the idea of a thirteenth column to represent our thirteen original states. This plan would be very amusing if there were not an element in it which may be very dangerous. The writer suggests that every one of us should appoint himself as a committee of one to listen to orators and others who express themselves in public. Each of these committees should then decide whether the speaker is abusing his right of free speech. Unfortunately, too many of us have different ideas of the meaning of free speech. Too many of us reserve the right of free expression for ourselves and deny it to others. I am afraid that the kind of thinking behind such a plan may lead to many troubles.

Ever so many people have written to me expressing a desire to take care of refugee children. Some of them want only French children, but it is quite obvious now that it is impossible to get these unfortunate youngsters out of France. Some want children from other countries which are equally impossible to reach at the present time. Everyone seems to feel that these children can be dropped into this country without the slightest difficulty. Unfortunately, this is not the case, but I hope that everyone who is interested in helping the innocent young European victims of the war will get in touch with the US Committee for [the] Care of European Children, which has been formed to bring children from England via Canada. Some of these children will be of other nationalities because they have left their native country to take refuge in England. There are many complications in bringing refugee children to this country with which the average person may not be familiar. The immigration laws have to be observed. Standards have to be set up for the homes of these children. There has to be supervision in each home to ensure good treatment and proper care. This is one piece of work which I am sure will absorb much of the energy now clamoring to expend itself in some service to the government.

In another letter which I have recently received, a well-meaning and public-spirited lady suggests that we undertake to increase our food supply by growing crops on every available piece of land. Such a suggestion may seem at first to have a great deal of value. But closer study shows that it does not take into account our complete national picture. I am afraid that this idea would not meet with the entire approval of the secretary of agriculture, because we now have surpluses of many types of food. There is an ample supply to meet the present or future needs of Europe as well as our own. This holds true even if many refugees can be brought here, although this does not seem likely at present. Because the food supply is so closely related to world trade, we cannot entertain the idea of growing more crops without considering the future of American exporting. If the war in Europe does not end soon, we will not be allowed to trade with the greater part of Europe. If the war does end soon, we still do not know whether any kind of general trade will again return to the world.

I want to be most careful in criticizing the suggestions which have been sent to me. It is a beautiful idea that we should plan ahead. It is wonderful that people all over the country should be thinking along these lines, but we should remember that much planning for the future has already been done. It would be a pity to waste our national energy in increasing our food supply, for example, when there is at present sufficient reserve to meet any generous impulse we may have or to engage in any kind of trade that may be possible.

To demonstrate further how some suggestions for our national welfare can misuse our national energy, I should like to tell you about another letter I have received. A lady suggests that we engage retired army officers to drill all the women in the country. Isn't it obvious that those of us who are able to cook would do better to improve our cooking than to learn how to be soldiers? National emergencies call for the best efforts of every citizen in their own special fields. I can see how calisthenics, or any physical development which would improve the health of our boys and girls and older people, might be valuable, for health is certainly one of the things which I think is a vital part of a defense program. And speaking of public health, it seems to me that many of us might put our minds to the problem of securing better medical care for all of our people, so that we would be better fitted to meet any unusual strain which we might be asked to endure.

One generalization which I might make about all the suggestions I have received in the mail is this: let us look to the improvement of

America and Americans first. For example, the tragedy which has come to the children of Europe is dramatic enough to appeal to people who have known little or nothing about the tragedy which faces many of our own children and their mothers and fathers in this country. I hope that bringing some of the refugee children to this country and placing them in various communities will serve to point up for us some of the conditions which face our own children. I can quite well understand the feelings of the people who say: "Why is there so much excitement about saving Europe's children when comparatively little has been done to save our own?" The answer, of course, is that the tragedy in Europe has come more quickly and is so forcibly brought to us through the press, radio, and newsreels—that it cannot be ignored. It must arouse the sympathy of a warmhearted nation. Many people can live a long while in a community and not know that nearby live other people who are in dire need. Perhaps those very people will become aware of the conditions that have remained hidden in their own communities, by seeing the conditions under which some foreign children live.

I know there has been a feeling of discouragement among many people because democracy achieves reforms slowly. But I still feel that this arises from a lack of knowledge, which keeps us as a nation from being really unified in our efforts to improve the democratic way of life. In other words, we do not know each other. We have ignored conditions which endanger democracy in our homes and in our own communities. But the brightest hope that I see ahead, and it may be a real salvation, is that the dangers which face us today may draw us together. The conflict in the world around us may force us to know our homes, our communities, our nation—and thus compel us to grow into a unified country, ever improving our democracy.

# 23.

# "Peace, Democracy, and Ideals"

*Mrs. Eleanor Roosevelt's Own Program*,
presented by SweetHeart Soap

Thursday, July 4, 1940

ER: Good day, ladies and gentlemen. I am extremely glad to be able to speak to you today from Hyde Park, because there are so many things to do here on this particular day. I don't know how I would have been able to find time for the motor trip to New York City. It would also have been extremely difficult to fit this broadcast into my husband's plans, because later today the president is going to turn over the papers for the new library at Hyde Park to the archivist of the United States. This will complete the acceptance by the government of this new building.

I have watched with great interest as this library has grown from a dream into a reality. And I certainly should like to be present at the last step. I shall be very happy when the exhibits are finally in place and students come to work with the papers which will be available for research work, and when people just drop in for a view of the various collections. There will be, I think, a Hudson River Room. Many naval items of historical importance from my husband's collection will also be included. Some of these will be loaned and some will be exhibited permanently. Part of the exhibit will be changed from time to time, so that everyone can visit and revisit the library always to find something new and interesting.

In England, at the Gladstone Library, they have built a small inn, not far away, where students may stay at a very reasonable rate until their work is accomplished. I hope that someday a similar arrangement can be made here, for I feel that this library offers a great deal of fine material which can be very valuable to students and writers.

The Fourth of July is not exactly a day of rest for any of us. When these semiofficial ceremonies of handing over the library to the government have been completed, we betake ourselves to the cottage and give our annual picnic for the newspapermen and photographers, who accompany my husband on this visit to Hyde Park. This is great fun, as I told you in last Tuesday's broadcast, and even if we all will be a little weary by the end of the day, it will be a satisfactory kind of weariness. I believe it is always worth getting tired when you are having a good time.

In the midst of what I am doing today, this thought flashes through my mind: How strange it is that we can go on during these days, living our usual normal lives, when only a few thousand miles away another nation—which has for many years celebrated its national holiday on July fourteenth—is now forced to face a completely changed status, and to start rebuilding its national life under very difficult conditions. I wonder whether we ever stop to realize, even for a moment, what it would mean to us if we were looking to a future as grim as the one which lies before that nation.

One of the things that I find most difficult these days is to keep a balance between ideals and realities. I am sure this problem is shared by a great many other people. Many have told me that they are prepared to defend our ideals of democracy and to preserve the American way of life. They are opposed to the Nazi, Fascist, and Communist forms of government. But all of this goes under the heading of ideals. Now, what about the realities? The same people who dislike dictatorships say that, above everything else, they do not want to go to war. They hope that conflicting ideas can in some way be reconciled without resorting to force. They cling to the possibility that the dictators will keep their activities out of the spheres of our interests. While I share these hopes most ardently, I feel that it is necessary to continue to face the facts. The economy of the dictators is different from ours. They never worry about what things cost. The life of the individual is absolutely unimportant. The rights of minorities have long since been forgotten. The peace of the neighboring neutral countries has been violated over and over again. Everything is sacrificed to the will of the dictator. Democracies, on the other hand, move slowly towards their objectives because they are unwilling to sacrifice human lives and human liberties.

If a dictator does not have raw materials within his own borders, he must be able to get them elsewhere. If he cannot get raw materials through trade he will get them by force. And force is justifiable in the dictator's philosophy. If we, as Americans, do not want to meet force with force, we must at least meet force with facts. As far as I can see, there are only two things that those of us who want a peaceful world can look forward to. One is complete disarmament. The other is a world economy which provides all nations, great and small, with an equal opportunity to secure basic commodities. I am not an economist, but this seems so simple to me as I view the world situation today. I am sure it is not simple to work out the details of either of these alternatives. I know that it will take the best brains of all the countries in the world. But the principle of giving the people everywhere in the world an equal chance to obtain basic commodities is the only way that I can see by which the causes of war can be removed. But such things as disarmament and balanced world trade are back in the realm of hope. The facts are that the dictators do not share the desire to work for the good of the world as a whole. As far as disarmament is concerned, they want everyone to disarm but themselves. As far as world trade is concerned, they want it at the expense of all the other nations.

We have a right to ask the question: Is such a thing as world peace really possible? Has there ever been a single instance in the history of mankind when individuals worked for universal good? I say there is. The field of science is a shining example of how the contributions and the genius of every nation have been used for the benefit of the entire world. The scientific viewpoint, which is completely unselfish, must become the viewpoint of governments and businessmen if we are ever going to organize a satisfactory world community. But until the world is more receptive to ideas for universal good, we must work furiously to preserve the good things in our own American way of living. We must not let the dictatorships outguess, outtalk, outwork, and outfinance us. And we believe that we can accomplish all of those things without sacrificing our democracy.

Our representative form of government was conceived on the principle that nothing shall be done unless the people consent to it. When the ideals of democracy were first formulated, the need was to slow down the speed of government. People were trying to build a defense against the lightning strokes of oppression at the hands of tyrants. Our forefathers thought that, whenever the people had enough time to slowly and coolly consider legislation, they would have a better chance to see that it was beneficial to all. That is why our Constitution balances the authority of one branch of the government against the other, and divides the legislative and executive powers among many people. Today, we must try to preserve that same machinery of democracy but to accelerate its pace.

This does not mean regimentation. It does not mean that all points of view should not be given consideration. But it does mean that we must be quick to realize what should be done for our national welfare. And we must be quick to act accordingly. The representatives in our government take their cues from us. If we are divided, if we disagree, they will act accordingly. But if we are as one in our thoughts and desires, we can match even the pace of one-man dictatorial government.

It is easy to say that we should speak with a single voice. But I am fully aware that this is not as simple as it sounds. I know that our economic system is completely satisfactory to some of us, and not quite satisfactory to others. How then, you may ask, is it possible for both groups to act unanimously? But there is a way. It calls for equal sacrifice by all; it calls for equal unselfishness; it calls for the farsightedness to settle the differences within our own country in order to achieve a common defense against outer forces, which are by far more important and more threatening.

At a time when outer forces are becoming more ominous each day, America is beginning a political campaign during which this country will be told what can be done to meet those outer forces, and how we should cope with our internal problems. We may deal with these issues in high-sounding phrases which mean nothing. Or we may come down to "brass tacks" and let the people know exactly what we face. I think we, as a people, have come of age and we are able to understand and be strong enough to face any eventuality. To say that we are going to have armament and not pay for it is ridiculous. To say that sacrifices will not be necessary from all is equally ludicrous. Rich and poor, big and small, every single American is going to have to do something personally, unselfishly, willingly, for the preservation of our democracy. But today, and throughout every day of the future, let us keep in mind these immortal words whose birthday we celebrate today: "We hold these truths to be self-evident: That all men are created equal. That they are endowed by their creator with certain inalienable rights. That among these are life, liberty, and the pursuit of happiness."

Upon our intelligence as a nation to understand these words, upon our willingness as a people to keep them alive, depends your future, my future, and the future of America.

# 24.

# "Address to the
Democratic National Convention"

July 18, 1940, 11:30 a.m. (NBC Red and Blue Networks)

In 1940, FDR decided to seek an unprecedented third term in office. He was ambivalent about running again. He had spent eight grueling years in office leading the country through depression and preparing it to defend itself against the Axis. Roosevelt had told confidants that he wanted to retire to his country estate in Hyde Park, New York. But with war closing in, FDR felt both an obligation and a desire to stay in command. ER also had mixed feelings about spending another four years in the White House. She found the role of a political spouse both constraining and, at times, tedious. But she did not discourage FDR from running. With war on the horizon, she felt there were few people qualified to succeed him.

FDR chose not to attend the 1940 Democratic National Convention in Chicago. There was little doubt that he would be nominated, but many of the party faithful in Chicago were in a sour mood over how Roosevelt's political lieutenants tried to manage the convention. ER and party chairman James Farley were at odds. The delegates were divided on a host of issues, including FDR's choice for a running mate, agriculture secretary Henry Wallace. A liberal idealist with shallow support in the party, Wallace was opposed by a variety of factions, including isolationists who feared that Wallace and FDR were keen to go to war.

The atmosphere at the convention grew increasingly ugly. Secretary of Labor Frances Perkins, who was at the event, phoned FDR and suggested that the first lady come to Chicago to help calm the waters. "I think she would make an excellent impression," FDR replied. "You know, Eleanor always makes people feel right."[1] ER thought the idea "utter nonsense" but she agreed to go.[2]

ER found the convention in turmoil and confusion. To her surprise, she was asked to address the delegates. The rowdy convention delegates grew silent as ER approached the podium. It was the first time a first lady had addressed a political convention. She kept her remarks brief. She told the delegates they should set aside their individual interests for the good of the party and the nation. "This is no ordinary time," ER said, as she encouraged the party faithful to come together. After she finished, the delegates nominated Henry Wallace for vice president.

ER: Delegates to the convention, visitors, friends: It is a great pleasure for me to be here and to have an opportunity to say a word to you. First of all, I think I want to say a word to our national chairman, James A. Farley. For many years I have worked under Jim Farley and with Jim Farley, and I think nobody could appreciate more what he has done for the party, what he has given in work and loyalty. And I want to give him here my thanks and devotion.

And now I think that I should say to you that I cannot possibly bring you a message from the president because he will give you his own message. But as I am here, I want you to know that no one could not be conscious of the confidence which you have expressed in him.

I know and you know that any man who is in an office of great responsibility today faces a heavier responsibility, perhaps, than any man has ever faced before in this country. Therefore, to be a candidate of either great political party is a very serious and solemn thing.

You cannot treat it as you would treat an ordinary nomination in an ordinary time. We people in the United States have got to realize today that we face a grave and serious situation.

Therefore, this year the candidate who is the president of the United States cannot make a campaign in the usual sense of the word. He must be on his job.

So each and every one of you who give him this responsibility, in giving it to him assume for yourselves a very grave responsibility because you will make the campaign. You will have to rise above considerations which are narrow and partisan.

You must know that this is the time when all good men and women give every bit of service and strength to their country that they have to give. This is the time when it is the United States that we fight for, the domestic policies that we have established as a party that we must believe in, that we must carry forward, and in the world we have a position of great responsibility.

We cannot tell from day to day what may come. This is no ordinary time. No time for weighing anything except what we can do best for the country as a whole, and that responsibility rests on each and every one of us as individuals.

No man who is a candidate or who is president can carry this situation alone. This is only carried by a united people who love their country and who will live for it to the fullest of their ability, with the highest ideals, with a determination that their party shall be absolutely devoted to the good of the nation as a whole and to doing what this country can to bring the world to a safer and happier condition.

# 25.

# "Shall We Arm Merchant Ships?"

*Over Our Coffee Cups,*
presented by the Pan-American Coffee Bureau

Sunday, October 12, 1941, 6:45–7:00 p.m. (NBC Blue Network)

Eleanor Roosevelt began the most significant series of her radio programs in fall 1941, as the United States was gradually being drawn again into world war. A year earlier, Congress had passed the first peacetime draft in the nation's history. FDR had asked Congress to approve a massive armament-production program to build 50,000 airplanes a year and to greatly expand the Navy. On December 29, 1940, FDR used a Fireside Chat to persuade Americans that the United States should drop its pretense of neutrality and become an "arsenal of democracy" by ramping up war matériel production to support Great Britain. Roosevelt also made a pact with British Prime Minister Winston Churchill known as the Lend-Lease Agreement. America would lend World War I–era destroyers to Britain, and in return Britain would lease certain military bases to the United States.

Eleanor Roosevelt's *Over Our Coffee Cups* program was sponsored by the Pan-American Coffee Bureau, a trade group representing seven coffee-growing Latin American countries. On this Sunday-evening program, ER commented on the week's news and interviewed guests. War naturally dominated much of the discussion on the thirteen-week series. ER also returned to themes she had developed in earlier programs, columns, and articles. She stressed that tolerance was essential to a healthy democracy, especially in a time of crisis. She called for free speech, equal treatment regardless of race or gender, the right to dissent, and the obligation of citizens to serve their country. On October 12, ER opened her program with a response to a speech made the previous week by Charles Lindbergh to an anti-interventionist rally in Fort Wayne, Indiana. The aviator charged that FDR had taken on dictatorial powers and was determined to plunge the nation into war. Lindbergh alleged that the president might even suspend the 1942 federal elections to prevent his adversaries from winning seats in Congress. "Such a condition may not be many steps ahead on the road our president is taking us," Lindbergh said.[1]

War in the Atlantic was on the minds of many Americans in the fall of 1941. German submarines had sunk more than 1,000 Allied merchant ships. In May 1941, a U-boat, acting without orders, sank the American merchant ship *Robin Moor* in the South Atlantic. The United States did not retaliate, but that summer FDR approved a plan to have Navy ships escort merchant traffic as far as Iceland. In September 1941, FDR responded to a U-boat attack on the USS *Greer*, a destroyer, by ordering the Navy to shoot at German U-boats on sight.

In her October 12 broadcast, ER commented on the recent sinking of a Panamanian tanker owned by a subsidiary of Standard Oil. The ship was transporting petroleum to a British port. Many of the men on board the *I. C. White* were Americans. Three of the thirty-seven man crew died in the attack. ER gave her listeners a humanizing picture of American merchant seamen risking their lives in the Atlantic. She said all Allied seamen, including two English boys she had met, "should be protected."

On October 19, 1941, ER commented on a Senate subcommittee investigation, led by anti-interventionist senator Burton K. Wheeler, a Montana Democrat, into the alleged production of pro-intervention films in Hollywood.

Civilian defense was a frequent topic of the *Over Our Coffee Cups* program. President Roosevelt had appointed colorful New York mayor Fiorello La Guardia to head the recently created Office of Civilian Defense (OCD). The agency's mission was to lift home-front morale by enlisting local volunteers across the country to strengthen and defend their communities. OCD volunteers conducted blackout exercises, filled sandbags, and established air-raid response plans. ER was persuaded by La Guardia's aides to take a position as an assistant director for volunteer coordination in the OCD. ER was especially interested in using her authority to see that women had meaningful work to do defending the home front. It marked the first time a president's wife had been given a federal appointment. ER's job would produce a lot of headlines, many of them critical.

ER wanted to use the OCD to provide local communities with social services such as child care and health programs, in addition to training local airplane spotters and civilian firefighters. ER believed that civilian defense depended on healthy communities. Maurine Beasley argues that ER "saw civil defense as an instrument for the continuation of progressive social legislation, which she feared would be forgotten in the present emergency."[2] On December 8, 1941, the day after the Japanese attack on Pearl Harbor, ER flew with La Guardia to the West Coast. They were there to inspect civilian defense preparations and to ease public fears about a rumored Japanese attack on Pacific Coast communities. During the tour, ER posed for news photos with Japanese Americans and used her newspaper column to say that the treatment of Japanese citizens would be "perhaps the greatest test this country has ever met."[3] ER opposed the internment of Japanese Americans and had tried to convince FDR privately it was a bad idea. But once his decision was made she supported it publicly. Historians have found curiously little in ER's paper trail to explain her relative silence on an issue that she clearly felt strongly about. Beasley asserts that ER stayed quiet because "Franklin probably demanded it."[4]

Eleanor Roosevelt kept her OCD post for five months. She outraged Congress and got attacked in the press for staffing some OCD projects with friends or celebrities—including film star Melvyn Douglas—who got handsome salaries and were said to have Communist ties. She was ridiculed for hiring a dancer named Mayris Chaney to develop recreational programs for children in bomb shelters. Under fire, ER resigned the OCD position and used her February 22, 1942, *Coffee Cups* program to fire back at her critics, including newspaper columnist Westbrook Pegler.

When the thirteen-week series of radio programs ended, the Pan-American Coffee Bureau renewed for another thirteen weeks. In retrospect, it seems extraordinary that a president's wife would take pay from foreign governments—even friendly ones—in a time of war. The program's commercial segments made implicit reference to FDR's so-called Good Neighbor Policy of nonintervention and noninterference in Latin American affairs. The program also played off the recognition that, should the Axis powers seek a beachhead in the Americas, the first likely targets would be in Latin America.

ANNOUNCER: The Pan-American Coffee Bureau presents Eleanor D. Roosevelt's views on current events, *Over Our Coffee Cups.*
VOICE 1: Get more out of your work!
VOICE 2: Get more glamour!
VOICE 3: Get more fun!

ANNOUNCER: Get more out of life with coffee! And here's how Miss Elvira Lane, alert and charming stewardess of American Airlines' famous flagship fleet, gets more out of life with coffee: Miss Lane tells us, and we quote:

VOICE FOR LANE: "An airline stewardess has to be a sort of flying encyclopedia, whether it's how to feed a six-week-old baby or explaining radio direction signals. It's important for us to know all the answers, just as it's important for us always to be cheerful, courteous, and levelheaded. That's why I'm sure we're all such coffee drinkers. We find that coffee steadies our nerves and actually gives us the extra energy we need for our jobs. When the job is done, naturally, there's nothing like a good cup of coffee to pep a girl up and start her off on a happy evening of pleasure and relaxation. We air stewardesses surely do get more out of life with coffee."

ANNOUNCER: Another lovely lady, a motion-picture star, has a tip to give on how to be beautiful. We'll give you this glamour tip before the conclusion of this broadcast. But now the Pan-American Coffee Bureau's charming news analyst is ready to give you *Over Our Coffee Cups*, her weekly digest of world events. Mrs. Franklin D. Roosevelt.

ER: Good evening, ladies and gentlemen. Some of you may have read with tremors a speech made a short time ago in which it was suggested that in 1942 the citizens of this country would no longer be allowed to vote. As a consequence, of course, I suppose all rights and duties of Congress would have to be abrogated. So I am not surprised to see some dark hints here and there which suggest that the executive branch of the government will take all kinds of vital steps which in the past required the cooperation of the legislative branch, without that branch being given an opportunity to express an opinion.

On the other side of the ledger, in the hope that it may give some comfort to the worried souls, I should like to point out that the executive has just sent a message to Congress, and the sending of that message to Congress, it seems to me, is an acknowledgment that Congress has an equal responsibility to carry certain burdens *with* the executive.

The real value of debate in Congress, over any measure, is not only the clearing of the minds of the legislators themselves, for their final decision expressed in a vote, but the opportunity which debate affords the people of the United States to understand the points at issue and to make their own voices heard through their representatives.

In order to achieve this, there must be a real freedom of the press, however; not the kind of freedom which requires a reporter to write his story always with the emphasis on a point of view previously decided on by an editor or an owner, but the kind which permits a factual story and leaves the opinion and interpretation of the fact to the editorial page.

This recent message to Congress deals with things which are most important to the American people. We are producing many things for the use of the democracies fighting the Axis powers. We are sacrificing our time and our money to do it. We are reorganizing our lives to achieve certain ends. We do it with our eyes open, knowing what the price will be if we succeed and what it will be if we fall. We are now confronted with the question of whether we shall make every attempt to see that goods ships reach their destination, or whether we wish to continue to leave that in the hands of those who cannot do it as successfully as we can.

Shall we arm merchant ships? Shall we allow them to go into belligerent waters under our naval protection? These are the questions up for debate, and Congress should hear from the people. In a democracy, people do not only have the right to vote, they have the right to bring their influence to bear on their elected representatives.

The torpedoing of the tanker *I.C. White* has come home with special poignancy to us here in the United States, because the sailors were almost all our own citizens, living in this country. As you look down the list, the names might indicate origins in various parts of the world, but the addresses are nearly all on the East Coast of the United States of America. Though I find one man from West Texas. In the records of these men, there are many little stories which show that they had every realization of the risk they were running. It is interesting to note that Bernard Brady of New York City, for instance, had written to his wife from Cape Town, [South] Africa, asking her to send his sister, who lives in Vermont, $500 out of his $5,000 war risk insurance in case anything happened. He was a fireman, so his wife was much worried, as she knew he must have been belowdecks.

Julius Wojslawowicz is only twenty-one years old. This was his first trip, and he had signed up because he worked as a lead-man at the Brewster Plant in Newark, New Jersey, and had fallen ill from the effect of zinc chromate fumes. His doctor had advised a job at sea and his family heard from him in Curaçao that he was well and cheerful again. His family sat up all night praying that he and the others of the crew might be saved.

I saw two English boys in Philadelphia from an English merchant ship who seemed quite unconcerned. Men will go on sailing for distant ports, for that is the way of the sea, so they *should* be protected.

Speaking of national defense, many people would like to know whether the expansion achieved by our Army is actual or merely on paper. Just in case you haven't seen the figures given out by the War Department, I am going to quote some of them. In May 1940, the Army consisted of approximately 230,000 enlisted men, 13,500 officers, and about 225,000 National Guardsmen, only partly equipped and trained. And now the Army consists of over one million and a half men.

There has been much said about the need for mechanizing the Army, and some people have suggested that it was not necessary to train so much manpower if you had the necessary mechanized equipment. Unfortunately, even the most highly mechanized army must have trained personnel, and infantry still has its place in war, which is being amply proved in Russia today. Men, however, can be trained more quickly than we can produce many of the things which they need to make them effective as an army in the field. It was necessary to develop new methods of feeding, of caring for their health, and of clothing them. All of this has gone forward rapidly. The greatest advance has been made in the mechanized equipment. In July 1940, there was only a total of 29,867 vehicles on hand. A year later, the number had been increased by 100,000, and it is mounting rapidly. The production of tanks and of every type of armored vehicle has gone forward, and by the end of 1941, the armored force will be increased by 1,400 percent over the amount which existed in 1940. In the providing of airplanes, we had to make a decision: on sending abroad or keeping them here. So we concentrated on providing primarily the equipment needed for training. This has been done very successfully, and Assistant Secretary of War Robert Lovett recently declared, "I think for the first time, we're going to have available in the maneuvers aircraft of a quality which has no superior anywhere in the world." Quantity of aircraft is of course a secondary consideration, as long as it is necessary for our airplanes to go to the English and the Russians. But quality, we can emphasize even more.

In the *Antioch Review*, Mr. Max Lerner, professor of politics at Williams College, asks, "What is the armory of ideas that we require for this war?" And he proceeds to answer himself thus: "Quite summarily these: that democracy has in it untapped strength and unused expansibility, both in waging a war and in reconstructing society afterward; that the peace must be approached in the spirit neither of vengefulness nor forgiveness, but determined planning for more feasible ways of running a world; that economic settlements are required fully as much as political; that there must be substantial steps toward a world federal structure of some sort; and above all, that we do have a picture of a new world to guide those who are fighting and to hearten those who are enslaved."

That seems to me a pretty good statement to guide our thinking for the future.

Further, it is good to find not only the president, but the undersecretary of state, Mr. [Sumner] Welles, laying stress upon a future world economic order where fair dealing for all countries shall be the aim of the United States. This is the only possible groundwork for future peace. We must be happy that our State Department and the president agree on this important policy.

To turn for a moment to labor, a Labor government goes into power in Australia, and the head announces that it will not try to remake the life of the nation overnight. Probably everything will proceed in much the same manner as heretofore. We do not have to have a Labor government in this country to bring about the consideration of labor problems. In a broad sense, all of us are a part of the labor family of this country, because comparatively few of our people do not work in one way or another. However, for the benefit of some of our highly paid workers who feel that their colleagues with lesser incomes are ruining them by their demands, let me suggest that they note the fact that even a Labor government hasn't seemed unduly to disturb Australia.

Incidentally, I just recently received a letter from Atlantic City, New Jersey, giving me a union card in the hand-knitters union. I failed to ascertain whether this is a CIO or an AF of L union. But being a member of the Newspaper Guild, and of the Radio Artists, I think I am collecting union cards as some people collect honorary degrees!

Turning from labor to the professions, our medical profession might note that in New Zealand, they have created a system of free medical care which will begin to function on November first. Like many experiments, this is evidently one which will need revision and improvement with experience, but it may be a step in the right direction.

By the way, I was appalled to see in a dispatch from Vichy, France, that the death rate of children under ten was 45 percent above the last five years' average. It is attributed to the long famine. The report introduced "Armistice Skinniness" as a new medical term.

Now to close, for the good, cheerful, American note. I do not know how many of you know the Barter Theatre in Abingdon, Virginia, run by Robert Porterfield. I first became interested when I visited Abingdon because my father had lived there. This theater runs entirely on barter. The audience pays admission with goods: cows, chickens, eggs, pigs, milk—anything they have. The actors and actresses live in a hotel nearby and sustain themselves on the food brought in. There are many amusing stories about this theater, and I was interested to see an item in the paper which stated that Robert Porterfield told the State Advisory Committee on the Budget that one sow paid all the royalties on all the plays produced by the troupe. Mr. Porterfield said, "We kept that sow, taken in one night at the box office, and soon there was a litter of eight pigs, and then there was another and another litter, and we paid royalties with hams." He added an amusing story about the time he wrote to Mr. Bernard Shaw for permission to present his play *Candida*, and offered Mr. Shaw the usual ham in payment. In his reply, Mr. Shaw said he had no use for the ham as he was a vegetarian, but that he would consider spinach. He got the spinach!

ANNOUNCER: Thank you, Mrs. Roosevelt. And now for your listeners, here's a tip on how to keep beautiful, from Miss Jinx Falkenburg, Columbia Pictures star, featured in *Two Latins from Manhattan*. Miss Falkenburg writes us, and we quote:

VOICE FOR FALKENBURG: "The best way I know for a girl to look her best at all times is to eat the right things, get plenty of sleep, yes, and drink plenty of coffee. Why do I mention coffee? Because I've found that when I want to look fresh and, well, you might say, 'blooming in the evening,' coffee is really a wonderful help. After all, you look as well as you feel, and coffee makes me feel cheerful and peppy."

ANNOUNCER: Why not try a delicious, flavorful cup of coffee with your evening meal tonight? And see how much more you get out of life with coffee. Next week at this same time, the Pan-American Coffee Bureau will bring you another interesting discussion of world events by Mrs. Franklin D. Roosevelt. This is Ernest Chappell bidding you all good night.

ANNOUNCER: Don't forget this is National Doughnut Month, and coffee and doughnuts are just one more way to get more out of life with coffee!

# 26.

# "Freedom of Speech"

*Over Our Coffee Cups,*
presented by the Pan-American Coffee Bureau

Sunday, October 19, 1941

ER: Good evening, ladies and gentlemen. The moving-picture industry has been under investigation by a congressional committee. The question seems to be whether the producers have a right to present their own views through the plays they produce. I think it is permissible for Senator [Gerald] Nye, Senator [Burton] Wheeler, and Mr. [Charles] Lindbergh to present their views to the world, but I think it is equally permissible for all others. Why is one [form of] propaganda any different from any other? Freedom of speech should be accorded to all. A very great man left us when [Supreme Court] Justice [Louis] Brandeis died recently. Many people throughout the country have paid him tribute and will continue to do so. I have been thinking about him today in connection with this hearing or investigation of the motion-picture industry, for the two great liberals of recent years on the Supreme Court, Justice Brandeis and Justice [Oliver Wendell] Holmes have both had a word to say on the subject of freedom of speech. It is perfectly evident that allowing a citizen to say "yes" to the government is *not* freedom of speech. The real test is whether a citizen has a right to say "no." And that right we have had for 150 years and it is still ours today.

Justice Brandeis's remarks on this subject read as follows: "Those who won our independence by revolution were not cowards. They did not fear political change. They did not exalt order at the cost of liberty. To courageous, self-reliant men, with confidence in the power of free and fearless reasoning applied through the processes of popular government, no danger from speech can be deemed clear and present, unless the incidence of the evil apprehended is so imminent that it may be fatal before there is opportunity for full discussion. If there is time to expose through discussion the falsehood and fallacies, to avert the evil by the processes of education, the remedy to be applied is more speech, not enforced silence."

But there are certain kinds of free speech which are not really permissible. Therefore, this is the point made by Justice Holmes in delivering the opinion of the court in the case of *Schenck vs. the United States*: "The most stringent protection of free speech would not protect a man in falsely shouting 'fire' in a theater and causing a panic." In other words, every subject should be a matter for free and full discussion. But we have an obligation to point out to the people as a whole the fallacies of any statements which we disagree with. Both men are apparently agreed on this and there were never two men more deeply interested in the preservation of our basic freedoms.

In our present situation here in this country, there is no question but what we have the time for full and free discussion. Therefore, I would not curtail the expression of anyone's opinion. But I would make sure that equal opportunity is given for all sides to be presented, through every avenue of communication, press, and radio. Freedom for one side only is not true freedom.

A letter has just come to me from a correspondent who is much upset because the word "traitor," she says, is applied to everyone who opposes the administration's foreign policy. She never mentions, of course, that the opposition has applied the term "warmonger" to everyone who champions this policy. This type of name-calling is never confined to any one side, but it brings up the whole question of free speech. And I think we should recognize today that we not only do respect free speech and permit it in this country, but that on the whole we carry on our differences of opinion on a higher level than we did twenty years ago. If we compare the congressional debates on the Lend-Lease Bill last spring with those on the League [of Nations] Covenant in 1919, we will see how much we have gained in seriousness and how much less vituperation and name-calling there really is in these days. It is very difficult to be a consistent people, just as it is difficult to be a consistent individual. But in this matter of freedom of speech, I think it is important enough for us to try to see that there is complete freedom of discussion and to be consistent on that one point at least!

Now to turn for a moment to the subject of national defense. Last week I gave you some figures which had come to me about our Army. Today, I have acquired some about our Navy. There are still many men, as you know, who think that the ultimate victory in any world situation goes to those who control the seas. That is where commerce is carried on; that is the lifeline of civilization. And therefore, it is of interest to us that our Navy today is the most powerful in the world. Three hundred and thirty-eight combatant ships are in commission, and 353 more are building. The Navy has 273,315 enlisted men. The Marine Corps has 59,968 men. And with the officer personnel included, this figure will run upward of 350,000 men in all. Every branch of the service is putting special emphasis today on aviation, and the Navy has 5,000 trained pilots, 3,600 students, and it is estimated that by July 1942, the Navy will have a minimum of 10,000 trained flying naval officers.

The value of having an aviation arm which is attached to the Navy or to the Army lies in the fact that branches of the same service work better together because they are more closely coordinated. This expansion in the Navy has necessitated tremendous expansion in the Bureau of Ordnance. Navy yards and many other allied industries are absorbing almost all available skilled labor, besides demanding certain materials which necessitate giving priority as to delivery of materials for the defense program. Among the men in the Navy, the morale has never been higher. They are not having an easy time of it. Many of them spend weeks at a time patrolling in stormy waters. One of them wrote me about "a trip down the coast in the teeth of a storm which broke over the bridge and carried away some glass. All of us on board are tired but in fine shape and ready to meet any emergency." That means hard work, and when people say that this generation of young people have become soft, I feel like saying that it is not the younger generation which is soft. Instead, the older generation is soft for them, now and then.

I received a wire, for instance, from two mothers of boys in the Army the other day bemoaning the fact that their boys had been disappointed at the end of maneuvers by having their promised leaves rescinded on returning to their base camp. I can fully realize that any mother must have been disappointed, and the boys themselves must have been depressed. But we are growing up in the United States, and one of the things we learn as we grow up is to accept disappointments and to learn that the unexpected is part of everyone's existence. On the other hand, it is good to know that so much hospitality has been shown to our young Army men wherever they have gone on maneuvers, and that on the whole their health has been extraordinarily good.

In Washington, DC, we are getting a number of women in different government departments, all of whom have interesting jobs, but those who at the moment have been attracting the most attention are the two who are working in the War and Navy Departments. Mrs. Hobby, who is a young Texas newspaperwoman, is doing the kind of work which should reassure the families of the boys who are in camps or on maneuvers. The other one, Mrs. Lewis, does publicity for the Navy. Mrs. Hobby is telling families what happens to their boys while they are playing at what may someday prove to be a very grim and real game.

And speaking of things which are real and grim, I must say that the fires which have occurred in Cleveland, Ohio, and in Fall River, Massachusetts, lately—and which have destroyed so many materials destined for defense in this country or abroad—are most discouraging. Where there is a question of possible sabotage, it is quite evident that the FBI must be given every opportunity to find out what individuals or groups of people are responsible. Where it is a question of neglect in the observation of certain very important rules, I think public opinion should rise up and insist that such things must not occur. We resent losing materials which we are making sacrifices to produce when they are on their way across the ocean. How much more should we resent the loss of materials which occur through lack of care in the observation of fire protection rules?

This has been a pretty serious talk tonight, so I'd like to close with one word of real cheer, especially for the American housewife. Dr. M. Harris, who is directing the work of the Textile Foundation, says we are going to have wool processed in such a way that it will be just as warm as it ever was, but it will not shrink in the laundry. And the moths will not find it so enjoyable. This is good news to all of us who have been accustomed to having our woolens shrink and to find moths have riddled them when we take them out of storage in the fall.

# 27.

# "Propaganda"

*Over Our Coffee Cups,*
presented by the Pan-American Coffee Bureau

October 26, 1941

ER: Good evening, ladies and gentlemen. There is an extraordinary difference between the broadcasts sent out by the German government and the attitude taken by the commanders of German ships. The German High Command knows quite well what these German ships actually do. And yet they take the trouble to tell their people that the American reports of the sinkings should be regarded with "the deepest skepticism." And they state that several American reports, which are as true today as the day they were made, have been proved untrue. And because of that they cast doubt on the report of German sinkings of any American ships. This savors somewhat of the attitude of fooling one's self, and of telling people only what they would like to hear.

All the news that comes out of Germany today, whether it is private and confidential, or whether it is sent out to the world, seems to be a mixture of wishful thinking on the one hand, and on the other, an attempt to terrify the world by showing how utterly without mercy or regard for human life is the German führer. How, otherwise, can we explain the reports of sending numberless Jewish people from Berlin and other cities, at an hour's notice, packed like cattle into trains, with their destination either Poland or some part of occupied Russia? For the life of one German officer, fifty French people are shot. And the punishment for acts of rebellion against German rule in any country becomes more severe every day. The man who orders these cruelties stood before the tomb of Napoleon, so the story runs, and as he turned away, remarked, "Napoleon failed in conquering the world, but I will succeed." I often wonder whether he had ever read a Russian folk story, which has to do with Napoleon's attempted conquest of Russia.

The story runs thus: Napoleon, because he had no pity, could cry out "Bonapart-ay, Bonapart-ay," and the soldiers he had killed would rise up to fight for him. One day, however, he saw a young Russian lying wounded, and the young soldier said, as Napoleon went by, "Tell me one thing, Napoleander: why did you kill me?" And because the young Russian was not really a young peasant soldier but the archangel Ivan, the words he spoke haunted Napoleon. And though he pulled out his pistol and shot the soldier through the head, the words still seemed to follow him, repeated by all the young dead men who lay upon the ground around him. Napoleon could not sleep in his tent at night. And when the battle came the next day, his heart had become soft and for the first time, he felt pity. On calling for the dead soldiers to come to the rescue, he found they had deserted him because the human emotion of pity had destroyed his power over them, so Napoleon and his army were routed. No man can count forever on being so completely dominated by his dream of power that God will not enter into his soul and make him feel pity. The day will come for the führer, as surely as it came for Napoleon.

Here at home, our defense effort goes on apace. We read daily that new ships slide down the ways. New airplanes are turned out. And now the president has sent out a call to civilians to do their defense duty. He has proclaimed the time from November 11 to November 16 as Defense Week. November 11 is Armistice Day, and ordinarily we hold services thanking God for the peace that came on this day, and praying that war will never come to us again. This year, in addition to our usual services and the decoration of the graves of the dead who fought in the last war, we will use the day as a reminder that liberty is always worth preserving. And that defense, for us, means the preservation of the liberty we have, and the continuation of our efforts to improve democracy at home, and to make it possible for the rest of the world to enjoy the same freedom that we enjoy.

The civilian defense to which the president calls us is concerned with a great many sides of the life of our communities. Today we are still primarily thinking about the rise in the cost of living, which is being felt more and more in every community. The low-income groups suffer the most, for the percentage spent on foods grows greater. In other words, the smaller your income, the greater is the percent spent on food. Prices keep going up, and yet the House hearings on the Emergency Price Control Bill have been carried on in a leisurely fashion during the better part of three months.

In a war economy, a nation has to divert a great part of its resources and manpower from the making of peacetime goods to the making of instruments for war or defense—planes, tanks, guns, battleships, et cetera. We pay for this vast defense effort, partly out of taxes, but to a greater degree, the government borrows. There is plenty of work and wages and profits in the hands of the people, but the amount that people can buy is limited by the fact that production is largely in defense materials, which the people cannot use in their daily lives. So they compete with their wages to purchase those civilian goods produced only by non-defense workers, which means that prices shoot up, unless the government institutes some kind of price control. In ordinary times, when the price of an article starts to rise, manufacturers produce it in greater quantity, and the price comes down. But in a crisis like this, prices start rising on all sides. There cannot be greater quantities produced because industry's working practically at capacity on defense.

More plants cannot be built nor more machinery produced, because the materials needed to do this are used in the production of defense articles. So instead of stimulating more production, as might have happened in peacetime, speculation and hoarding begin, which results in taking supplies off the market, and prices go up. Workers attain higher wages. These wages are reflected in higher manufacturing costs. And make the article bought by the people more costly and the vicious spiral in prices and rising wages has begun.

We are still in the opening stages of the spiral in this country, but the Bureau of Labor Statistics reports that the cost of living on a national average has risen about 10 percent since the war started in 1939. Most of this increase has taken place in the last few months. Wholesale prices have risen over 22 percent. You wonder why this sharp rise in the wholesale price hasn't been reflected in the prices we pay in retail stores. That is partly due to the fact that the retailers have been selling off their stocks and haven't had to replenish yet. When they do, in the course of the next few months, this cost will be reflected in retail prices, unless some adjustments are made in the near future.

There are various ways of trying to check inflation. You can try to remove from people what excess money *they* have by taxation or by urging them to buy defense bonds. This latter suggestion of course will be of value in the future, because that money will be available for expenditure to stimulate private spending to start industry functioning on a peacetime production basis again. We can limit the amount and the terms on installment credit. But this method never seems to go far enough, and the method of volunteer cooperation to place ceilings on certain goods produced by industry and trade does not seem either to completely control inflationary tendencies. So it would look as though the only thing that remains to be done is to pass some kind of legislation which will fix the ceiling for prices in an effort to be fair to buyers and sellers both. There is naturally an appeal made when prices are controlled to control wages. But it seems unfair on the whole to put human labor and commodities in the same category. The Fifteenth Amendment to the Constitution makes many people doubt whether doing so might not be in certain instances classed as involuntary bondage.

It would seem to be better, perhaps, to protect the worker from the rising cost of living, not only through control of the price of foodstuffs, but through some kind of rent control. And then appeal to his democratic patriotism for a voluntary stabilizing agreement arrived at by the machinery instituted for collective bargaining.

I have wanted for a long time to find a real instance where people bothered to lie to prove their own ideas. And lo and behold a letter has just come to me from the Pacific coast which gives me my proof. My correspondent says that in practically every city he visited, stories had been told to the effect that the largest Jewish-owned department stores had discharged many American workers in order to provide jobs for Jewish refugees. No story could tend to create disunity more rapidly. And it *is not* true. It might be the time for a seasonal lay-off, or any one of a number of reasons might make a drop in employment temporarily necessary. The Germans circulate a story like this to create a dislike of the Jews. I sometimes wonder if it would not be well to organize a committee called American Unity to explain that creating rifts between various groups is not the way to promote goodwill, because sometimes it acts as a boomerang.

# 28.

# "Isolationists"

*Over Our Coffee Cups,*
presented by the Pan-American Coffee Bureau

November 16, 1941

GEORGE HICKS: The Pan-American Coffee Bureau, representing seven Good Neighbor coffee-growing nations, presents to you American families your Sunday-evening visit with Mrs. Franklin D. Roosevelt. During the past week Mrs. Roosevelt made another of her famous flying trips, this time into Ohio and Michigan. Two great states in the heart of America's glorious Middlewest. What sentiment did Mrs. Roosevelt find there about the present crisis in our international affairs? What are her answers to the Middlewestern isolationists? This evening, Mrs. Roosevelt has graciously consented to tell us.

ER: Good evening, ladies and gentlemen. As you have said, I was in Michigan and Ohio last week, and it was a flying trip, Mr. Hicks, just as you called it.

GH: Well, in your brief talks with people in the Middlewest, Mrs. Roosevelt, what reaction did you find to the problem of national defense?

ER: I was in Michigan and Ohio, and I think this is probably one of the centers of strong "America First" sentiment. This I believe is partly because of the leadership and partly because—while they are a defense production center—they feel themselves far away from the coast and find it impossible to visualize any attack from Europe or Asia. It seems practically impossible from their point of view.

GH: You were telling me, though, that some people in that part of the country did take the threat to their security very seriously, even to the extent of publishing a Hitler invasion map of the Middlewest.

ER: Yes, Mr. Hicks. Someone told me that there had been published in this area a rather interesting map, superimposing Russia on our own map, and showing that the German Army's successful march toward Moscow would mean practically a march in this country reaching to Indianapolis, Indiana, with such cities as Cincinnati being wiped out on the way.

GH: And what's the answer of the isolationists of Ohio and Michigan to this map, Mrs. Roosevelt?

ER: Their answer is probably that the German Army did not have to cross an ocean to get to Russia and did not have to land in the face of opposition. All of which, I grant, adds to the difficulty of invasion and does give one a measure of security.

GH: But Mrs. Roosevelt, what would be your answer to those in the Middlewest who feel themselves geographically secure from attack from Europe or Asia?

ER: Well, suppose we forget temporarily about the traditional way of fighting a war and think about the possibility of a new kind of war. Suppose Hitler is able to subdue the whole of Europe, including Great

Britain. That would give him control of the seas and the ability to produce ships, both for war and for commerce, far beyond our own ability
to do so.

I have heard people ask why we cannot make peace with Hitler. Why
can't we do business with Hitler? The answer is contained in a little book
called, *You Can't Do Business with Hitler,* which everyone should read.
If Hitler controls the seas, he can outbuild us, and we need no further
proof of his organizing ability. He would control as slaves a great number of people, and he can undersell us.

You do not have to land an army on our coasts. You can fly today and
do more harm with bombs than any army could possibly do. Doubting
Thomas, complacently secure, will say, "Where are our airplanes?" They
will be out trying to defend our shores as the boys of the RAF [Royal
Air Force] are trying to defend England. And both sides will lose men
and planes. If we cannot outbuild and out-train the waves of men and
machines that come over, we eventually are going under.

GH: Those are very serious and thought-provoking words, Mrs. Roosevelt. You believe, then, that every citizen, whether he lives on the East
Coast, on the West Coast, or right in the center of this great country of
ours, should face the same stern facts?

ER: Yes, I do, Mr. Hicks. There are two possibilities every citizen
should ponder, because they are the two things that all of us are up
against today. First, we are either going to furnish material which makes
it possible for nations now fighting Hitler to win out, regardless of what
it costs us. Or we are going to find ourselves eventually fighting alone,
with all the resources of Europe and Asia against us. Too great a sense of
security has caused the downfall of many nations, and sometimes I wonder if we do not suffer in high places from too great a sense of security
now, and too little realization of the sense of insecurity which prevails
among certain of our people.

GH: You mean economic insecurity, Mrs. Roosevelt?

ER: Yes. Those people may think that there is nothing worth risking their lives for since it seems to them simply a transfer to a new bondage, which may be better than the present one and which they believe cannot be worse.

That brings me to the second possibility I mentioned a moment ago. We are going to make our communities worth living in through the work of volunteers in our civilian defense work. Or if this work is not particularly glamorous, and we cannot find volunteers who will take it seriously and put it through, then we are going to have groups of people who do not think our land is worth defending. That situation would give Hitler the most valuable ally he could possibly have.

GH: Then, Mrs. Roosevelt, you believe a great factor in civilian defense must be increasing the effort on the part of the individual community to see that its own people are taken care of—that there are no persons in that community so underprivileged that they can see nothing in the American way of living to defend?

ER: Yes. Our federal agencies which gather information on relief report that in many parts of our great country there are families lacking food, shelter, clothing, and many other things which we count as necessities for healthful and decent living, simply because the community has no money or too little money to provide needed general relief. Poverty breeds physical and mental disabilities and, finally, delinquency. While we have every reason to expect that the rising tide of employment will mean that people are able to pay for a better standard of living, it will not excuse us from doing the work which will educate them to take the best possible advantage of any change that may come in the employment picture. This must be done by the communities that are aware of the situations they face.

GH: But Mrs. Roosevelt, haven't the relief agencies been counting on surplus commodities to help feed the unemployed?

ER: That's just it, Mr. Hicks, Those surplus commodities may disappear completely in the next year. Then we shall have a very serious social situation. In thousands of cities, towns, and villages and country places, there are still families who are unable to get enough relief for even the barest necessities of life, if indeed they can get any relief at all. In fact, there is one great state where the relief workers are accustomed to stories which run something like this: "I am hungry and my kids are hungry. We haven't had anything but surplus [food] for so long I am too weak to look for work. And I don't know if I could hold a job if I could get one. The flour and beans are good, but they just won't last us a month." And this state is no exception. This is truly a national problem of defense to be met in communities from coast to coast.

GH: That's very serious indeed. Mrs. Roosevelt, we have received many letters, as we know you have, asking for more of those delightful stories of yours like that story you told us last week about Princess Juliana and her little daughters. I know you've brought us another story or two from your trip.

ER: Flying from New York City to Detroit the other day, we had an amusing pilot who passed word back to us that we were on flight eleven on the eleventh day of the eleventh month, that his license was one-eleven and it was the eleventh year of his employment with the American Airlines. We were on route seven, he added, for the benefit of the superstitious who could feel that seven and eleven was a good combination. Altogether, the coincidences on eleven, I thought, were quite amusing.

Last week I told you about those two little Dutch princesses. Well, the children of this country are certainly becoming conscious of their importance as citizens. Two small boys came to the door of our rooms at the hotel in Detroit, demanding to see me. Miss [Malvina] Thompson explained that I was busy and could not see them, and then the smaller one said, "But we belong to the American public, too, and we want to see Mrs. Roosevelt." You can be sure Miss Thompson let them stay and made me stop and speak to them.

And now, I would like you all to bear in mind the creed written by Stephen Vincent Benét for those who work in civilian defense. A voluntary pledge:

I pledge myself as an American to the work of civilian defense.

I do so voluntarily, in faith and loyalty, because I believe in my country.

I believe in its freedom and its greatness, in the liberties I share with all Americans, in the way of life we, the people, have made here with our own laws and with our own hands.

I mean to defend those liberties and that way of life, with my own hands, here and now. The task I am called upon to do may be small or large. I mean to see that it gets done.

It may mean hard work and sacrifices. I mean to see that it gets done.

I am neither soldier nor sailor but, as an American citizen, I take my place beside the armed forces of the nation, willing and ready as they are to protect the homes and the lives, the wellbeing and the freedom of my fellow citizens, to defend the country I love, to maintain its cause against all enemies and every danger. And to this task I pledge my whole strength and my whole heart.

Now, Mr. Hicks, before I close, I want to call attention to the fact that the American Red Cross roll call is now going on, and everyone who is not a member of the Red Cross will be given an opportunity to join. And those who are annual members can rejoin between the dates of November eleventh and November thirtieth. Surely there is no one who would not want to give this organization whatever support they can at this time, when the Red Cross is sending help all over the world.

GH: Thank you, Mrs. Roosevelt, for your inspiring discussion of world events, for your charming stories, and thank you for speaking for that great institution, the American Red Cross. Next week, we understand Mrs. Roosevelt has invited to be her guest on this program Mr. Daniel G. Arnstein, who has just returned from China's lifeline, the Burma Road, where his recommendations for traffic control have already increased the flow of war supplies to China. Until then, good evening, and don't forget that good-night cup of coffee.

# 29.

# "Pearl Harbor Attack"

*Over Our Coffee Cups,*
presented by the Pan-American Coffee Bureau

December 7, 1941

Radio flashed the news to the nation at 2:30 p.m. Eastern time: Japanese airplanes had attacked Pearl Harbor. The radio networks cleared their schedules to provide rolling coverage throughout the day. Industry was warned to be on guard for sabotage. Servicemen and -women were ordered back to base. The Navy announced that all recruiting stations would open at eight the next morning. One newspaper described the attack as "the biggest news event in U.S. radio history." [1]

Eleanor Roosevelt's regularly scheduled NBC news commentary program, *Over Our Coffee Cups,* was scheduled for that evening. ER went from the White House to NBC's Washington studios with her secretary, Malvina Thompson. When she arrived, ER told the advertising agency man in charge of her program that she had been rewriting her script. A newspaper reporter turned Army morale officer named Jimmy

Cannon was her scheduled guest. Cannon fumbled with the clasp on his script and ER calmly leaned over to help him.

The first part of ER's message was directed at the nation's women and youth. "We know what we have to face and we know we are ready to face it," she declared. ER inaccurately reported that the Japanese ambassador had been talking to FDR at the White House at the time of the Pearl Harbor attack. She had mistaken a Chinese diplomat for Japan's ambassador. Then, ER introduced Corporal Cannon and spoke to him about troop morale. After the broadcast, Cannon remembered walking the streets of Washington, "feeling big and proud because on this night I had been in the presence of the president's wife."[2]

ANNOUNCER: This is Leon Pearson speaking for the Pan-American Coffee Bureau, which represents seven good neighbor coffee-growing nations, and presenting to you American families your Sunday-evening visit with Mrs. Franklin D. Roosevelt. This evening Mrs. Roosevelt has as her guest Corporal James Cannon, 1229th Reception Center, Fort Dix. But first, Dan Seymour has a word from our sponsors, the Pan-American Coffee Bureau.

ANNOUNCER DAN SEYMOUR: In this moment of trial, the seven neighbor countries which make up the Pan-American Coffee Bureau welcome the chance to express their support for their great good neighbor, the United States. The new solidarity which has been effected between the Americas in the last few years stands us all in good stead in the face of this emergency. This applies not only in a commercial sense, for Uncle Sam can count on Latin America for essential materials, whether oil or tin or copper or coffee—but also in a political sense. The Americas stand together.

PEARSON: Thank you, Dan Seymour. And now here's the Pan-American Coffee Bureau's Sunday-evening news reviewer and news maker, to give us her usual interesting observations on the world we live in, Mrs. Franklin D. Roosevelt.

ER: Good evening, ladies and gentlemen. I am speaking to you to-night at a very serious moment in our history. The cabinet is convening and the leaders in Congress are meeting with the president. The State Department and Army and Navy officials have been with the president all afternoon. In fact, the Japanese ambassador was talking to the president at the very time that Japan's airships were bombing our citizens in Hawaii and the Philippines and sinking one of our transports loaded with lumber on its way to Hawaii.

By tomorrow morning, the members of Congress will have a full report and be ready for action. In the meantime we, the people, are already prepared for action. For months now, the knowledge that something of this kind might happen has been hanging over our heads. And yet it seemed impossible to believe, impossible to drop the everyday things of life and feel that there was only one thing which was important: preparation to meet an enemy, no matter where he struck. That is all over now and there is no more uncertainty. We know what we have to face and we know that we are ready to face it.

I should like to say just a word to the women in the country tonight. I have a boy at sea on a destroyer. For all I know he may be on his way to the Pacific. Two of my children are in coast cities on the Pacific. Many of you all over this country have boys in the services who will now be called upon to go into action. You have friends and families in what has suddenly become a danger zone. You cannot escape anxiety. You cannot escape a clutch of fear at your heart. And yet I hope that the certainty of what we have to meet will make you rise above these fears.

We must go about our daily business more determined than ever to do the ordinary things as well as we can. And when we find a way to do anything more in our communities to help others to build morale, to give a feeling of security, we must do it. Whatever is asked of us, I am sure we can accomplish it. We are the free and unconquerable people of the United States of America.

To the young people of the nation, I must speak a word tonight. You are going to have a great opportunity. There will be high moments in which your strength and your ability will be tested. I have faith in you! I feel as though I was standing upon a rock. And that rock is my faith in my fellow citizens.

Now we will go back to the program which we had arranged for tonight. I spoke to you a few weeks ago on the subject of Army morale. I suggested one of the best ways to make the boys in our armed forces more contented with their lot was for the people at home to really do their duty in the various activities of home defense. This evening, I wish to discuss Army morale again, but this time in an even more concrete and specific way. And that's why I am delighted to have as my guest a young man who is a member of our armed forces, Corporal James Cannon of Fort Dix. How long have you been in the Army, Corporal Cannon?

JC: I've been in six months, Mrs. Roosevelt.

ER: You were a selectee?

JC: Yes, Mrs. Roosevelt.

ER: Well, after six months of Army life, how do you like it?

JC: I want to tell you, with great sincerity, I am proud to be a bad soldier in this great army of the people.

ER: I don't believe you're such a bad soldier, not with those stripes on your arm, Corporal Cannon.

JC: Honestly, Mrs. Roosevelt, I'm not so hot. But there are good soldiers in my outfit. By the way, Mrs. Roosevelt, do you know who had the highest score in our outfit when we shot for score? A fellow who used to play a pipe organ in a roller-skating rink. He'd never held a rifle in his hands before. But competent instructors have made him a sharpshooter in less than a year. And I'll bet there are men like him in every Army post in America.

ER: Then you feel from your personal observation—and after all, you *are* a trained newspaperman—that the Army is making civilians into good soldiers?

JC: Mrs. Roosevelt, in the six months I've been in, I've seen a miracle take place. I've seen ordinary, easygoing guys turned into efficient members of a powerful fighting force. That's what's taking place in every training base in this country.

ER: I am sure that's true, but let me ask you a rather personal question. Aside from actual military training, do you find you are learning anything which is of value to you as a person, as a citizen?

JC: Mrs. Roosevelt, I'm glad you asked me that question. I think I speak for hundreds of thousands of us in training camps everywhere when I tell you that the Army has given me a completely new set of values.

ER: You certainly are an honest soldier. Can you tell me just how the Army has given you this new set of values?

JC: I was born and raised a New Yorker. I used to think America was a suburb of New York. I had the New Yorker's contempt for people who lived beyond the Hudson. Now I soldier with a lot of guys from the brambles and the bushes and the whistle-stops. And I find they can do a lot of things I can't do. Sure, I can write a fair piece for a paper or a magazine. I can get wisecracks in a Broadway column. But I've neglected myself physically. I've gone soft. It sounds corny, I suppose, but you know I've learned to respect these guys from the sticks. They aren't wisecrackers, but they're tough, strong kids. They're good soldiers, and I'm proud to be soldiering with them. When it comes to a showdown, they'll be ready to make the sacrifices to preserve the American way of life.

ER: I am sure that there are many men like you, Corporal, who are learning the greatness of America and the greatness of their fellow

Americans perhaps for the first time. But surely, there are things which you don't like about the Army?

JC: I don't like those hikes. My feet tear and blister. I can't like getting up in the dark of the morning. I'm a clumsy chambermaid. My bed always looks like a haystack. But these discomforts are small. I've had a lot of laughs in the thirty-two years of my life. I'm willing to kick back one or two years so that I can live the rest of my life with dignity. I feel ashamed of the grumbling I've done, the complaining about the little, unimportant things. Because at this minute, soldiers of our Army are proving that, under fire, they are true and brave and worthy of the trust our democracy places in them.

ER: Corporal, do you find an interest among the men in the Army in the present world situation?

JC: I'm on Captain John Parker's morale staff, attached to the 1229th Reception Center, Fort Dix. I talk to the guys when they first come into the Army. Up to now, the only things they were interested in was: Where were they going to be shipped and if they were on the list for kitchen police. I'm certain all that will change now. When I left camp, we were a peacetime Army. Now we are the Army of a country that has been attacked. But all of us, all of them, have a very definite opinion on the Army in the state of the world.

ER: And what was that opinion?

JC: They know they are in the Army because we have had no choice here in this country. They realize that all we Americans have lived for and died for will vanish from the Earth unless we have a strong Army. Their philosophy is this: We were minding our business. They picked on us. Well, we'll show 'em.

ER: I think your answer is a very good one to those who would question the morale of the Army. Speaking of morale, what would you suggest to the average civilian as the best way in which they can be helpful to the men in the service?

JC: You'll have to excuse me if I give a pretty strong answer to that question. First, the civilians can cut out those stale jokes and stop that mocking salute too many of them hand a man in uniform. Let them give a soldier the dignity he is entitled to. Tell them to treat a soldier as you would a civilian; let them go unnoticed. The same fools think it is their privilege to break into a group of soldiers in a restaurant and violate their privacy. Tell them to cut out calling a soldier "Sarge." The same guys call a Pullman porter "George." We're a civilian army. We're the army of the people. And we want to be treated that way.

ER: I hope that our listeners will take your words to heart, Corporal Cannon. To sum up then, you think that democracy is working in our new army?

JC: Not only in the Army but right here. Where else, where else in the world would a guy like me be able to talk to the first lady of the land?

ER: Thank you, Corporal Cannon. I am sure we are training a very gallant army as well as a brave one. Now I see that Mr. Leon Pearson is anxious to ask me some questions.

LP: Yes, Mrs. Roosevelt, there are some very important questions I would like to ask you. First, of course, is this: Have you any comment to make on the strike bill which passed the House of Representatives?

ER: Well, Mr. Pearson, there will not be any more strikes. But it was interesting reading the editorials in the *Herald Tribune* and the *New York Times* on the bill. I think the wisest suggestion made is that the Senate should limit any legislation of this kind for a period of six months. The *Times* editorial stressed the fact that certain parts of the bill seemed ill considered. But I think there is a more important reason than that for limiting the period for any kind of labor legislation which is passed at present. Until legislation is actually on the statute books, we cannot tell what effect it will have in practice, nor can we tell at present what conditions we will be meeting in the months to come. Therefore, like so many other things, it's hard to make a blueprint to meet unknown needs.

LP: Mrs. Roosevelt, there's another question I'd like to ask.

ER: Yes, Mr. Pearson?

LP: A lot of writers and commentators are criticizing the government for not letting the people know enough about what is actually going on in public affairs. What would your reply be to these critics?

ER: Thursday morning, Mr. Pearson, Mr. Walter Lippmann published what to me was a most interesting column on this subject. It was interesting not because of the facts alone but because in the light of present-day happenings, he interpreted some of the difficulties which have faced responsible people in government during the past six months. I think that most of us should take to heart this kind of explanation, for many times responsible people are accused of not telling the people of the country enough, or not taking them into their confidence. Yet, if they did so, it would probably be the greatest show of weakness that any leader could make. It's always easy to blurt out all you know, to try to get your burden shared by other people. It's far more difficult to take the best advice you can get, make your own decisions, knowing that you will only be adding to the risks of the situation if you try to turn the decision over to others who cannot have the same background and knowledge.

LP: That is certainly a candid answer to the question, Mrs. Roosevelt.

ER: I would add one other thought along the same line, Mr. Pearson. It's interesting to note how carefully the Axis powers sugarcoat any bad news which they have for their people. I hope the people of this nation always are strong enough to accept the bad news and still keep up their courage. That is one thing about Mr. Winston Churchill's treatment of the British people for which I have the greatest admiration. He expects them to meet bad news with complete fortitude. And the mere fact that he expects it brings the proper response.

LP: And now, Mrs. Roosevelt, we understand you spent part of this week in New York City. Were you Christmas shopping?

ER: Yes, I did some Christmas shopping. And one afternoon I found myself in a crowded elevator in a large department store. Suddenly, a lady near me seemed to have a brainstorm and, looking at me, she asked, "Are you Mrs. Roosevelt?"

"Yes," I said.

And she then proceeded with, "Do you mean to say you go around without any guards?" I thought there was nobody left in New York City who would be surprised at meeting me almost anywhere at any hour of the day or night. So I was quite shocked to find that I was looked upon as a curiosity when found in broad daylight in the elevator of a large store

LP: And Friday, I understand, Mrs. Roosevelt, you graciously received at the White House the charming young ladies who are representing my sponsor, the Pan-American Coffee Bureau, in a goodwill tour of this country?

ER: It was a great pleasure to meet these young women from Latin America who are here on a tour of goodwill. And I hope they enjoyed their cups of coffee in the White House.

LP: I am sure they did, Mrs. Roosevelt. And now, speaking of coffee, Dan Seymour, I understand you have a word or two to say on that subject.

DS: I certainly have. The seven young ladies who, as guests of the Pan-American Coffee Bureau, have come from their republics to enjoy a visit with leaders in public and social life in the United States, are delighting everyone with their charm. Just as coffee, the delicious product of their homelands, delights more and more of us every day. Next week at this same time, Mrs. Roosevelt will be with us again to give us more of her interesting views on world affairs.

This is Dan Seymour saying good evening for the Pan-American Coffee Bureau. And don't forget that good-night cup of coffee.

ANNOUNCER: Now, more than ever, do your part—buy defense bonds and stamps.

# 30.

# "Civilian Defense"

*Over Our Coffee Cups,*
presented by the Pan-American Coffee Bureau

December 14, 1941

ANNOUNCER: This is Mrs. Franklin D, Roosevelt's regular Sunday-evening broadcast, sponsored by the Pan-American Coffee Bureau, representing seven Good Neighbor coffee-growing nations. As you know, Mrs. Roosevelt last Monday flew to Los Angeles to engage in active service on the front line of national wartime civilian defense. This evening, speaking from Seattle, Mrs. Roosevelt has many important facts to tell you about the first week of civilian defense in an America which is learning the reality of air-raid alarms and blackouts. She also has very real suggestions as to the work you can do in this great national emergency. So we shall take time to say only this about our sponsor's product: Coffee gives the extra energy every one of us needs in times like these. Coffee gives extra steadiness to nerves strained by high pressure and hard work.

Coffee, more than ever before, is America's necessary drink. And now we proudly present Mrs. Franklin D, Roosevelt.

ER: Good evening, ladies and gentlemen. It's very difficult to talk to you about current events because things are happening so rapidly it's almost impossible to keep up with them or to interpret them.

There is one thing which I can tell you which is rather a personal incident, but which I think will indicate the general attitude of people throughout the country. When the news came of the bombing of Hawaii and [Civilian Defense] Director [Fiorello] La Guardia and I both realized that civilian defense on the West Coast would, at once, become a more urgent question than it had been in the past, we decided to leave last Monday night for the West Coast. Our purpose, of course, was to find out what we in the central office in Washington could do to be useful to individual communities throughout the country. And we wanted to have an opportunity to meet with the state and local defense councils to see how plans which had long been made would be put into actual operation. We felt that if a good pattern was laid down in one part of the country, it would be helpful to us in stimulating similar activity in other places.

We found a condition which was not surprising. Like many other communities throughout the country, plans had been made, but very few citizens had felt any compulsion to agree to new taxes in order to actually put themselves on a war basis. We are a peace-loving people and have never wanted war. And it has been almost impossible to feel that we should prepare ourselves for that eventuality. Now that it has arrived, a change has come overnight in the psychology of all of our people.

In Phoenix, Arizona, after the [false] broadcast about the air raid on San Francisco the night before, two boys leaning over a fence at the airport looked at me quite casually in the early morning hours and said, "You're on your way to a dangerous part of the country, Mrs. Roosevelt."

There was evident envy in their voices. The old spirit of adventure hasn't left our people.

The first meeting of the local and state defense councils which we attended in Los Angeles impressed upon me some very simple things. I think we need to get every region of the country to publicize at once, in every possible way, the simple things which every citizen needs to know. For instance, what constitutes an air-raid warning. These warnings should be uniform throughout the country, because as people move around they should not have to discover what new signals mean. What constitutes an all-clear signal. What are the things you do in your own home—immediately, today—to ensure the least discomfort in a blackout even if you think you're not going to have any blackout. It will do no harm to prepare and put on a test to be sure that you can comply with the rules if you have to. There should be one room in every house where there can be light without it shining through. This can be achieved by hanging a black curtain through which light cannot shine over the window. If you cannot buy that kind of black cloth, you probably have old curtains or even a rug which you can adapt to this purpose. Perhaps that room should be the kitchen, since you may have to cook and you cannot do that in the dark. Almost everything else can be done without light. Remember that even a match is visible from the outside and can be a guide for a plane in the air.

Learn certain definite things. Stay in the house. Pick out the safest place for the family. Do not stay near the windows. Know where your young children are at all times. Make your plans for them in an emergency, so that neither you, nor they, can be taken by surprise. Do this in conjunction with school authorities. Do not feel that tomorrow is time enough. Do whatever you have to do today.

I spent Tuesday evening at Occidental College in Los Angeles. It is among the first colleges to establish a war council, set up just as a city's defenses should be. Students and faculty are assigned to all the occupations and services which they would undertake in any locality. Our colleges have an important role to play in training our young people for whatever jobs they have to do on leaving college. I was very happy to have this opportunity to meet with representatives of student bodies of many colleges in the vicinity of Los Angeles, and to sense the fine spirit among the young people, who desire to be of service as soon as called in a military way, but, immediately—now—in civilian defense, wherever they may be. One boy, who has been rejected by the draft board for physical disability, came up to me and asked what other occupations were open because he felt he must be of service. He asked, "Would there be any government jobs in minor positions where I could be of use?" I'm sure he is typical of all our young people. This question seemed to me something which the colleges should explore immediately, for they could prepare boys physically unfit for Army service in other ways where they would undoubtedly be very much needed.

It was in Dr. Remsen Bird's living room at Occidental College that a group of us listened to the president's [Fireside Chat]. I could visualize the scene in Washington, and I agreed fully with one of the guests who said to me afterwards that he liked the calm acceptance of disaster, the conviction of a long, hard strain ahead, and the quiet assurance which rang out in that voice. It came to us clearly, like a vital personality across the radio waves, saying, "In the end, the people of the United States will win out, and decency and civilization *will* continue in this world."

On Wednesday, I went to San Diego by train because the weather made flying impossible. We met with the defense council and I had a very short visit with our son John, who is on active duty in the Navy. His wife had been ill, and I do not think her recovery is helped by the fact that all of her own family are in Hawaii and she has had no word from them. It was on the train Wednesday morning that I read our first war-casualty list. It's many long years since I scanned those lists, and I knew with what anxiety many people through the country have waited, and continue to wait, to be finally saddened by the certainty of the loss of some member of their family or friends. Those of us who lived through the last war have been picturing what this meant to all the people in the belligerent countries for many months past, and now it will be a part of our daily existence. It is impossible for the president or for me to personally tell each and every family how deeply we sympathize in what they are going through. But if any one of you listening have lost some near relative or friend, I want to say to you how much I hope that you will cherish, with pride, the memory of the soldier or sailor who dies in action. In some way, bitter as the loss may be, you may be helped to bear it by thinking that he has joined the long procession of men through the ages who have fought to preserve humanity and freedom.

Director La Guardia and I separated in Los Angeles. He went directly to San Francisco, while I went to San Diego. Thursday I spent with the defense councils of San Francisco and the metropolitan area. One thing has come out of this experience—namely, the realization that the two sides of civilian defense, the protective and the volunteer participation, must work together. They meet and overlap at so many points. Air-raid wardens, for instance, are the focal point of much of the protective work. In preparation for an air raid, they must use, however, all the community services available for the people of the area. The air-raid wardens take training under the Army or the police force, but they must choose assistants from the people working in the various community services. Otherwise, they cannot build up strong defenses to keep the kind of morale which will stand up under a long strain.

The civilian-defense volunteer bureaus, which are under the local defense councils, are the center of the community, and feed to every community the needed volunteers for both sides of the work, choosing those best suited to do whatever kind of work is needed. These bureaus must be prepared to find the answer to every question asked by civilians, to provide training for people who desire it, to see that no need of the community goes unfulfilled because of not being able to find the right person to do the job.

Friday we spent in Portland, and went to Seattle that night. We drove from Seattle to Tacoma on Saturday for a civilian defense council meeting, and today we leave for home. It has been a joy to be here, for even a short while, with my children. In every place, I've found the Red Cross well organized and fully prepared to meet the demands which may be made on them. In preparation for any eventuality, they must of course expand and increase their supplies. So I hope that everyone in the country will make some contribution to the new $50 million war relief campaign which is now on. Give as much as you can so you can have the satisfaction of knowing that you have done your share to alleviate the suffering of your fellow citizens.

In closing, I want to remind you that tomorrow, December fifteenth, is Bill of Rights Day. I was to have spoken from New York City on a radio broadcast in celebration of this extremely important occasion. The president will speak to the nation tomorrow evening, and so I need not emphasize what this day and this celebration means to us as a people. I do want to urge each and every one to get out a history book and read the Bill of Rights. For in it, there are principles which we must live up to during these trying times if we are to preserve our freedoms. Every American citizen, regardless of race or creed or color, has a share in these rights, and it is the duty of every one of us to preserve them. Because if we allow them to become meaningless for any of our citizens, they will become meaningless for all of us.

# 31.

# "Preparedness for War"

*Over Our Coffee Cups,*
presented by the Pan-American Coffee Bureau

December 21, 1941

ER: Good evening, ladies and gentlemen. There is one thing about the American people when any emergency arises. It seems to spur them on to greater activity, and the more difficult the task may be, the more ready they are to meet the situation. I imagine that is a trait common to all virile people. I've noticed many times that there are people who lose interest in anything the minute it becomes easy to accomplish but who will work untiringly as long as the problem before them is challenging. Perhaps this is a trait of the American people as a whole.

In any case, the realization that we are actually at war and that we have a tremendous problem to solve—because we are completely making over the trend of thought which the majority of our people has built up for the past twenty years—does not seem to faze us in any way. Instead of being cast down, we seem to feel that this is a challenge to our ability to adapt ourselves and still not give up the main objectives for which we've been working through the past twenty years.

A short time ago, I am sure the vast majority of the people in this country hoped that we would not get into the war. If we faced the disagreeable fact that we probably would have to come in at some point, we did not think of it in concrete terms, neither as war with Japan nor as war with Germany and Italy. If anyone said we might go to war with Japan, the attitude was always that we would be so superior to the Japanese that poor little Japan would be wiped off the map. We were very cocky. Or perhaps we were just ignorant. In any case, it has the same effect, because it lulled us into a state of mental and spiritual unpreparedness. So remote did it all seem that we never faced what a victory for the Axis powers might mean, even if it was only a victory in Europe, with Europe dominated by the Axis powers and their ideas.

What would it mean to us to have, just across the Atlantic, a whole continent of people who did not believe in private industry, who did not believe in trade unions, who did not believe in the rights of the individual to life, liberty, and the pursuit of happiness? At least, they would not be allowed to express their beliefs if they retained them. There would be a whole continent of people subservient to the idea that the state is paramount and that their führer, whoever he may be, is next to God, in fact, practically takes His place. And that, by right of birth and ancestry, their race should rule the world. Ideas spread, and it would not take very long for these ideas to cross the ocean. We know how easily small groups of Fascists, Nazis, and Communists in this country have influenced the thinking of some of our citizens, and yet we lulled ourselves to sleep with the idea that a whole continent could be bent on making these theories succeed, and we would be left to pursue *our* interests and develop *our* friendships with *our* neighbors on *this* side of the ocean, untouched and uninfluenced.

We look back now, and this frame of mind seems incredible.

Suddenly, the Japanese planes flew over Hawaii and our other island possessions, and it gave to the American people an entirely new realization of what the world in the future, dominated by Axis methods and ideas, would really be like. And overnight, we were a people welded together, no longer divided; one great united people for the period of the struggle.

Nothing exemplifies this more clearly than the Industrial Labor Conference, which met this past weekend and which was addressed by the president at its opening session. He said to these gentlemen that he has asked them to come together to help win the war, as they were as important in this effort as the men in military uniform. The president further said that two moderators would preside over the group, one from the executive and one from the legislative branch of the government, and that he hoped they would achieve a complete agreement and, above all, speed. He wanted as much speed in turning out materials in the defense industries as he expected from the armed forces of the nation. Fortunately for us, we are geographically very well located. Our territory is so great that it is hard to concentrate on aerial attacks in the way which has been done in England, on such cities as London, Plymouth, Manchester, or Glasgow, Scotland. Production has got to rise in this country to tremendous heights, because we have the ability to produce, and at greater speed than any other nation in the world. The president talked to management, as well as to the workers.

An effort will of course be made by the enemy to take us, again, unawares—to raid some city where there is a big defense industry. And when these attempts are made, they will have two objectives: one, to slow up industry and, two, to break civilian morale. Being widely scattered over great stretches of territory is an advantage to us. It also has disadvantages, however, because of the fact that it will be easy to spot a city and to attempt to attack vulnerable points, using the same methods which they've used so well in the past. People rarely worry about what is happening to them as long as they are not directly hit. But they worry immediately about what may be happening to their families. Therefore, it will be part of the tactics of the attacker to wreck as many workers' homes as possible. There are only a comparatively few people in management. Their homes are not easy to find. But there are a great many workers, and because they live close together, the production can be greatly slowed down if the workers leave their machines to find out what has happened to their families.

It does not mean that we can expect the impossible of people, given an attack. We cannot expect that, if word comes that certain parts of the city are damaged, the people whose families live there will remain at work and not go to their rescue. We can do all that is humanly possible, however, to keep ourselves on the alert and prepare for this type of attack. Our people can know what to do when air-raid warnings sound. If they leave a house where they have little protection, they can find new places of protection nearby which are somewhat more substantial. My friend, Lady [Stella] Reading, writes that night after night she has slept under her heavy dining-room table. And I gather that if you're weary enough, and accustomed enough to air raids, you can even sleep through the noise and confusion of a blitz! The president went on in his speech to point out that this means a complete self-discipline and putting aside of personal interest. Every one of us is going to have, he said, a personal "must."

Young Captain [Colin] Kelly, who dove his plane onto a Japanese battleship, had no orders to sacrifice his life in that way. It was his own personal "must." And that is how, in one way or another, all of us are going to meet situations in our work and in our lives. Labor and management were asked for a quick agreement to speed up production. They were told plainly that the war is serious, that we've not won it yet, that civilization is at stake for the rest of the world as well as for us, and that we have a responsibility to maintain and increase our capacity as the arsenal of the civilized world.

That same obligation rests on every government worker, on every individual carrying on his own job day by day. He must make it a better job so that the community in which he lives will be strengthened thereby. It rests on every housewife of the country to run her home a little better and to meet her difficulties with ingenuity.

We are a very fortunate nation, even at war, because as far as we now see, we will have no shortage of food or of clothes. To be sure, we may not have the variety we've had, and I should not be surprised to see great standardization go into effect on many things. But we will have the wherewithal to keep ourselves warm in winter, [not] like the German people who have been asked to sacrifice all warm clothes for the Army. We will have shelter. We will have all the real essentials of living. Many people in other parts of the world will go without these essentials or have them rapidly and drastically curtailed. As individuals, we will hope to remember the Chinese proverb which the president quoted to the gentlemen in industry and labor: "Lord reform thy world, beginning with me."

Last Wednesday afternoon, when I faced the students of many South and Central American countries and a few European countries, I was strangely moved at the thought of what these young people are facing at this Christmas season. And as we approach this Christmastime in a world racked with war, I'd like to remind you again to make your donation to the American Red Cross. This great organization is making a drive for $50 million to carry on the tasks which they know the next year must bring. Their job will not be easy, so do your part by making a substantial contribution. Make it as your Christmas gift to a suffering and bewildered world, for I think that you will agree with me, the Red Cross, more than any other group, lives and works by the simple words that have come down from the first Christmas: Glory to God in the highest, and on Earth peace, goodwill toward men.

Somehow it's difficult to think, or to really have much Christmas spirit this year. And yet, in the deeper sense, we should all of us try to emphasize the spiritual values which have made this celebration live through the dark ages. In a world where "Love Thy Neighbor" seems to have lost its real meaning, and where consideration for little children is as academic as learning a dead language, we must still remember that everything we fight for today is typified in the Christmas story. And that though we may not have a merry Christmas, we must still have a hopeful one. And someday this present orgy of hate and war will come to an end. And then there must be somewhere in the world a flame of love, burning brightly enough to give the people of the world confidence to fight for a new order, in which peace, and goodwill, will be permanent.

# 32.

# "Enemy Aliens and Women in War Work"

*Over Our Coffee Cups,*
sponsored by the Pan-American Coffee Bureau

Sunday, February 15, 1942

ER: Good evening, ladies and gentlemen. There are several subjects in particular which I would like very much to discuss with you this evening: The problem of what we call "enemy aliens," the question of women in war work, and the problem of national carelessness.

Concerning the first subject, I think it is unfortunate, indeed, that we have to use a phrase because it is traditional—namely, "enemy alien"—when we talk about the people in our midst who are not citizens and who came to us from other lands. We know that we have enemy aliens, and we want them apprehended and put where they can do no harm, but we also know that we have innumerable friends who are aliens, who have taken refuge in the United States and whose whole hope for the future lies in the justice and the freedom which this country offers.

It is obvious that many people who are friendly aliens may have to suffer temporarily in order to ensure the safety of the vital interests of this country while at war. It is well, I think, to tell the Japanese and our own people some facts: namely, that the government agencies are in control of the situation; that the Army and Justice Department are fully cooperating; and that it is most important to stabilize employment conditions in West Coast industries.

I want to point out here that private vigilante activities, while they may be inspired by the highest sense of patriotism, may jeopardize the national security and bring retribution against thousands of American nationals in the Far East. It is much wiser and safer to leave this whole situation in the hands of legally constituted agencies, reporting to them anything which seems suspicious.

We are going to move the Japanese population out of strategic areas on the West Coast as soon as possible, but it is going to be done so that they will not waste their skills. They must not be allowed to plant their gardens and then have to leave them, because those gardens are not only a source of subsistence to them, but they supply many people in the United States with vegetables. They should plant gardens where they are to be moved in order that we do not have an unnecessary economic strain upon the country.

This is just one incident, but there must be many others, and all of them must be dealt with on the community level. So, it is important that you and I, in our communities, study the problem of the alien, the citizen born in another country, or the citizen born here but of foreign parents, and try to deal with this problem with all due regard to the safety of the nation—never forgetting, however, that the things for which we fight, such as freedom and justice, must be guaranteed to all people and not to just a select few.

Now for the question of women in war work. Today saw the starting of the registration of older men up to forty-five under the Selective

Service Act. I am sure there are many men for whom useful and necessary occupations will develop in the course of our war effort, which will take them out of the work which they are doing at present. I do regret, however, that women are not being registered at the same time as men. I feel quite certain that if the war lasts long enough, we will register women and we will use them in many ways, as England has done. I think it would save time if we registered women now and analyzed their capabilities and decided in advance where they could be used, if they are needed and as the need develops.

We are trusting, of course, that women will volunteer wherever they can find useful occupations, but this seems to me to be a rather wasteful method. If Selective Service is of value where men are concerned, it should certainly be equally valuable where women are concerned. I have already received many letters, from high school girls on up to great-grandmothers, who recognize the fact that they can find or make jobs for themselves in various fields of service and that they can go on performing the service which is most important at all times—running a home to the best of their ability when they have one. But many people have none. They are the ones who most vociferously are demanding that the government list them and evaluate their capacities and put them where they can be of most value.

People who have trained themselves or who have a gift along certain lines can always be used to advantage in their specific field. Some are likely to neglect this consideration in their desire to be of service and volunteer to do some work where their previous training will be of little value. This is wasteful, and we should eliminate the waste if we possibly can.

It may be possible, of course, to get a very good picture of the woman-power of the nation, if this is available in the volunteer offices established under the local defense councils. However, this will never be as complete as a government tabulation of the type undertaken in the mobilization of manpower.

Incidentally, I was reminded very forcibly the other day of the need for more women in the nursing profession. My third son was on leave from his ship in order to have his appendix removed. He came through his operation successfully, so there was no cause for anxiety. But when I visited this child of mine in the hospital, I went through some of the wards with the doctors and realized how urgent a problem is the recruiting of more women for the nursing profession. For we are using so many more nurses now in the Army and Navy that the Red Cross has made an appeal for girls to take up this profession. Even during their period of training, they will be making a contribution to the winning of the war. Whether they continue in the profession after the war or not, this training will be of value in their homes and in their community life.

Again I would like to make the suggestion that people who cannot see their way clear to giving full time to training in the nursing profession, can still give time enough perhaps to become a nurses' aide. The Red Cross course for nurse's aides requires a given number of hours of academic and practical work, and at the completion of the course a number of hours of volunteer service in a hospital. And this will give women and girls who can give three or four hours a day, every day, a chance to become a nurse's aide. These nurse's aides will relieve the trained nurses of many minor duties and make it possible for them to give the skilled care which makes so much difference in the recovery of the patient. Nurse's aides also can do much of the watching of patients, which is very valuable in critical cases, and yet they will allow regular nurses to go about their duties with a much freer mind, for they know that someone with a certain amount of training is watching at the bedside of a patient who might need emergency care.

There is also, of course, the field covered by the regular Red Cross workers who have long provided a much-needed hospital service by writing letters for the men and by intelligently contributing to their entertainment, and thus making their convalescent period more cheerful.

These ladies are a link with the families who cannot be at the hospital because of distance or their financial situation.

Now, as to the great problem of our national carelessness. The burning of the [ocean liner] *Normandie* this week and its final capsizing [in New York Harbor]—in spite of all the efforts made to minimize the fire damage—probably will be celebrated as a victory in the Axis countries. Whether this fire was caused by sabotage or not is perhaps unprofitable to discuss. But I think there is a serious lesson for all of us in this fire, and the fire which will delay the finishing of the Hotel Statler in Washington. That lesson is one of taking great care about little things. We, as a nation, are apt to be careless. We throw our matches down without making sure they are out. We drop cigarette ashes without paying attention to whether a living spark still burns. We do not always grind out our cigarette stubs. Every one of these little careless habits may bring us a fire, and once a fire starts, it is hard to say how much damage will occur. We are all familiar with the fact that we lose thousands of dollars' worth of trees every year because of the carelessness of hunters and campers and passing motorists. Let us resolve, as a measure which will help us to win the war, to be careful of little things, as this has a bearing on our national habit of waste.

We're going to need things not only for ourselves but for the benefit of our allies all over the world—food and clothing and vital war materials of every kind. It will astound any family if they start to save in little ways, how much it will amount to in a week or a month. The delay in the use of the *Normandie* is important for all of us, because our production can be speeded up to the nth degree in this country. But it achieves its maximum value only if we distribute what we produce throughout the world. So the protection of convoys and the sliding-down-the-ways of merchant ships are as important as the production of the things which we use for the protection of the United States.

I have been surprised to have people write to me that they were not able or willing to buy defense bonds or stamps for one reason or another, and their arguments have been based on the premise that they were giving something to the government. Every stamp and bond will be redeemed at the stated time, and every investor in these bonds and stamps will receive his or her money back, plus interest.

Now, in closing, I would like to leave you with this thought: When any public man says that we should consider only our own needs—that we should have done this in the past as well as in the present—it shows how little he understands the magnitude of the world situation. He shows, above everything else, that he has learned nothing from world events in the past few years. We can no more live in a world that is alien to our form of government and our way of life than we could stay out of war and remain unattacked in a world which was at war. Only men with vision to embrace the whole world picture are of any value at the present time.

One of the things which we must keep before us is the fact, also, that we must not only fight this war side by side, but we must learn in doing so to get on with other people—to recognize the fundamental qualities in other people which put them on our side. We may be irritated with an individual who remarks that, because we tried to stay at peace and have only just come to fighting beside him, we're playing a less important role. But our own irritation at this criticism is not of great importance. The thing we must be sure of is that this individual is fighting for the same democratic rights in which we believe. Otherwise, the Atlantic Charter will not mean anything. The war will have been fought for nothing. As we fight side by side with the men of China, of India, of Africa, of Great Britain and its dominions, of South America, of Russia, of the Netherlands, and of Norway, and of the other countries who are our allies, we must make it our job to know what are the fundamental things which will preserve a free and democratic world. Yes, and we must make sure that those who are with us are our true allies, in the important sense that they believe in the fundamentals of democracy and of freedom.

# 33.

# "Answering Her Critics"

*Over Our Coffee Cups,*
sponsored by the Pan-American Coffee Bureau

Sunday, February 22, 1942

ER: In the past week, Singapore has fallen and a fight took place in the Channel in which two Nazi battleships, in the fog, took a desperate chance and made port. They were apparently much damaged, but the British lost a number of planes, which meant also a number of young lives lost. In spite of these heartbreaking and important events, more time was spent in Congress, over the air, and in the newspapers, discussing what would seem to be relatively unimportant things. As these things have been made so important, however, and as some members of Congress have seen fit to make me of greater importance than I have ever before thought I possibly could be, I am taking this opportunity to explain to those who listen to my broadcasts why I think civilian mobilization is necessary on two fronts.

No one will question the advisability and the importance of

protection, as far as possible, of property and human life against possible air raids and fires. But many of us realize that this protection will be uncertain and inadequate if it consists only of a concern for blackouts, the training of more policemen and more firemen, and the providing of more emergency medical care. In the long run, the strains that we, in this country, will have to endure are the strains of uncertainty. Anxiety for loved ones far away, anxiety for ourselves in case of attack; the stress of the need of greater production, which will require longer hours of work and less loss of man-hours of labor because of illness and accident; the inclusion of women in the program of production, with the adjustment in our everyday living to sacrifice; and discomfort which we have not had to bear in the past. This necessitates, I think, better nutrition, better housing, better day-by-day medical care, better education, better recreation for every age. Day nurseries and nursery schools must be established where needed. Organized recreation must be provided for every age, but particularly up to working age.

And now to meet the explicit attacks which have been made. I have resigned from the Office of Civilian Defense and I am, therefore, free to speak my mind as a private citizen. I suggested Miss Mayris Chaney's name to the director of physical fitness, who appointed her at a salary which was fixed by responsible authorities for the work which she was expected to do. I suggested her because I thought she was qualified to do the work on a program which she herself had worked out and thought might be of value. I believe in physical fitness and I think it is important for the nation as a whole, no matter where the program is finally carried on.

I should like to quote what Dr. Jesse Feiring Williams, of the Department of Health and Physical Education and Recreation, Teachers College, Columbia University, has to say on the subject: "But let no one suppose that physical exercise is for youth alone. It is the basis of active vigor in all persons. Our duty seems to be clear. It is to keep fit today, not only for the better individual lives which we can live, but also for the better service which the nation so sorely needs." I believe that dancing— not fan dancing, which was just a slur put in for the sake of clouding the issue—but rhythmic dancing, ballroom dancing, folk dancing, have a place in physical fitness for young and old.

As to Mr. Melvyn Douglas, it seems to me that we in this country should have a feeling of deep gratitude to the writers, actors, artists, and musicians who always give so generously of their time and talents to charitable and civic institutions of the nation. It is apparently all right for businessmen to come to Washington to give their services on an expense basis, but not for an actor. We should be grateful to these businessmen, and we should be equally grateful to men like Mr. Melvyn Douglas. Generosity of money and time and talent is something for which we can be grateful. But [just] because people have fought and stood for liberal causes, they need not be branded as communists in this country, which gives us freedom to be Republicans or Democrats, reactionaries or liberals.

I do not want a program which I consider vitally important to the conduct of the war, and to the well-being of the people during a period of crisis, to suffer because what I hope is a small but very vocal group of unenlightened men are now able to renew, under the guise of patriotism and economy, the age-old fight for the privileged few against the good of the many. Perhaps we must all stand up now and be counted in this fight. The virtuous Westbrook Peglers on the one side, the boondogglers, so-called, on the other. But I think if the people of this country can be reached with the truth, their judgment will be in favor of the many as against the privileged few.

This is not a question of Republican or Democrat. It is a question of privilege or equality. I am resigning because I do not want to bring on a good program, and on good and valued public servants, the attacks and criticisms which are bound to be made on some of us in this fight. But if there has to be a fight, I am glad I am enlisted as a common soldier with the many.

There is nothing which those people who have raised this hue and cry can give me or take away from me that matters in the least to me. What makes this country, in the long run, a better place in which to live for the average citizen, what makes us strong to win the war and the peace, is because our needs are met and because we are given a sense of security that matters. For that I intend to fight.

# 34.

## "Broadcast from Liverpool"

Sunday, November 8, 1942, 9:15 p.m. [British time]
(British Broadcasting Corporation)

In September 1942, Eleanor Roosevelt was invited to visit Great Britain by Queen Elizabeth. The United States had been in the war for nearly a year and thousands of American troops were stationed at bases across Britain. But the Anglo-American alliance was strained. The United States was fighting, in part, to spread democratic ideals around the world; British Prime Minister Winston Churchill, meanwhile, hoped to survive the war with his nation's colonial empire intact. Some Britons complained that Americans had little idea of the suffering they had endured in three years of war. There had also been tensions among British and American troops on the island. The trip naturally posed some danger to the first lady. Although there had been a lull in the German bombing of London, the possibility existed of further raids. But FDR and his aides saw the potential political and diplomatic value of the journey. ER was keen to make the trip. After being forced from her job at the Office of Civilian Defense, she was looking for new ways to contribute to the war effort.

ER's mission was to tour war-damaged Britain and let the people of both sides "know a great deal more about each other."[1] She also wanted to report back to women in the United States on the condition of their husbands and sons stationed there, and on how the everyday households of Britain were coping during war. ER and her secretary, Malvina Thompson, flew to England as guests of the king and queen. ER stayed with the royals at Buckingham Palace, then toured cities and the countryside to inspect bomb damage and home-front initiatives. ER was in the media spotlight throughout the three-week visit. Her boundless energy and exhausting itinerary through factories, schools, hospitals, shelters, and military bases left a number of British reporters footsore and breathless. Crowds cheered and clapped when she appeared. Throughout the trip, ER and Thompson filed copy for the daily newspaper column back home.

As her trip drew to a close, ER made a radio broadcast to the British people over the BBC from the city of Liverpool. She urged her audience to think about the work to be done once the war was over, how to go about winning the peace. Her talk followed the popular nine p.m. news bulletin. The head of the BBC told an American diplomat in London that ER's speech drew an unusually large listening audience—some 51.4 percent of the adult civilian population of Great Britain. The *Times* (London) praised ER's "indomitable spirit" and ventured that her "eager sympathy and warm understanding have brought her into close contact with every section of the population."[2] Churchill was delighted with ER's trip, sending her a note that she had left "golden footprints" behind her.[3]

When ER returned to the United States, she continued to write and broadcast about her experiences across the Atlantic. She delivered a number of national radio talks on wartime conditions in Great Britain over NBC.

ER: Good evening. First of all I should like to thank the people of Great Britain, who everywhere have given me such a warm and sympathetic welcome, and to rejoice with them on this momentous day. I also want to thank the many kind people who have written me. I have not been able to answer all of these letters but I am nonetheless appreciative.

I realize that I am here as a symbol, a symbol representing an ally whom the people of Great Britain are glad to have fighting with them. Not only because we bring them material strength, but because the peoples of the two countries feel that they are fighting for the same objectives—a world which shall be free from cruelty and greed and oppression, a world where men shall be free to worship God as they see fit, and to seek the development of their own personalities and their own happiness within the limits which safeguard the rights of other human beings to do the same.

The peoples of our countries know that they will never compromise in this fight. But they also know they must plan, now, to establish a method of working together for the future. Without such cooperation among all the united nations, we cannot hope for the kind of world in which it may be possible to maintain peace.

I have only a short time tonight and so I can only sum up for you quickly the impressions which stand out as a result of the days which I have already spent here. I am sure that I will learn much more in the remaining days of my visit.

First, it seems to me that the women of Great Britain have assumed their responsibility in the war in a truly magnificent way. From top to bottom, for men and women alike, among the representatives of all the united nations whom I have met here, material things seem to have found their level and to be no longer of primary importance. A man said to me the other day that he had heard of the loss of a substantial piece of property belonging to him and it seemed such a trivial matter that, for three days, he forgot to tell his wife. Before the war, he said, it would have worried him for days, and now it meant nothing.

It means nothing because people have seen bricks and mortar disappear. They have found that it did not really matter—that they could rejoice if those whom they loved were safe. The nearness to catastrophe enhances, enormously, this sense of the value of personal relationships. A woman said to me quite blithely the other day, "We have all accepted the fact that we may be destroyed at any moment, so danger has no meaning to us." This spirit is the spirit of the people as a whole. If all of your possessions are destroyed, it really does not matter whether they were contained in one room or in twenty rooms. What you have left may be only your determination to go on fighting for the rehabilitation of the world. But that is important. That seems to live as long as those you love are about you.

People seem to have come through unbelievable hardships, smilingly. The people of Great Britain have learned to meet emergencies. I had an emergency meal the other day, such as would be supplied in a blitzed area. It was quite as good as one that you would eat in many a private household.

There is great gratitude on every hand here for the generous gifts received through the Red Cross, the Bundles for Britain, the British War Relief in America, and from cities and individuals. People who might have been cold have been clothed with garments sent from America. People have been fed from mobile canteens and rescued in ambulances sent from America. And last but not least, the American Army and Navy and Air Force are making friends here. Some of our soldiers helped in the harvesting, and since then they have preferred to go back to visit the families with whom they worked rather than to go to the town in their time off. Such men as have been stationed for any length of time in an area have found hospitable people. Hospitality is not a matter of sharing food these days, for the British, high and low, live on a food ration. If they give any of their rations to our men, they have to go without and sometimes they do. But there is so little excess they cannot do it often. For everyone—man, woman, and child—on this island is working and needs must eat his ration.

The work of the women is what I was asked to come here to study. I haven't the time to tell you tonight in detail all I have seen, even along these lines, or my full impressions. But I hope to have the chance to tell the American people later. I have seen that the women are working side by side with the men in the military forces, in industrial jobs, and in addition, they are doing countless numbers of jobs in civilian defense, as volunteers with the Women's Voluntary Services. They work, as well, in many of the long-established organizations like the Red Cross, the Y's, the Women's Institutes which in the rural areas make the wheels go round.

One valuable thing that seems to have been learned is not to duplicate work, but to leave to each organization the field that it can cover best, realizing that there is plenty of work to be done and that it is only a matter of finding where you can best function as an organization or as an individual. I have seen no woman who is not doing a real job, requiring in many cases a full eight hours' work a day, as well as carrying on full-time or in a modified way whatever her job had been before the war.

The working woman in some cases is confiding the care of her child or children to the day nurseries in the cities, or to the full-time nurseries in the country. Sometimes this is done for the good of the child, sometimes because the mother needs the added money to keep the family going while the man is away in the service, and also because the country needs her work.

To the mothers, wives, and sweethearts of our men, whom I have been seeing in different parts of Great Britain, I can only say that the men are doing their part extremely well in adjusting to a climate which is traditionally in November somewhat rainy, and so has given them plenty of rain and mud to cope with under conditions which require a saving of fuel and therefore an endurance of cold which we know nothing about in the United States of America. Added to this, they have had to learn to live under blackout regulations, of which no one in the US has the slightest conception. A blackout here is a total blackout. The countryside loses all of that friendly feeling which twinkling lights that shine out of a window give you as you walk along a country road in the dark. Here, a country road is a dense blackness. A passing car is a black object with two tiny lights. In the cities you carry a shaded torch. And should your torch gleam too brightly, a policeman—he is called a bobby over here—will soon tell you what changes you must make. This is a quality of blackness which no one who has not known it can possibly imagine.

But your men folks will keep their American sense of humor, their buoyancy of spirit. They have good times. They sing as they play and as they march. I have been to hospitals, and even those who are going home because for some reason or other they will not be able to fight again have the courage to face it with a smile, whatever their burden may be. American women can be proud of their boys over here. I imagine most of them would tell you that they would give a great deal to be home again. But every one of them, I am sure, will do his part and do it gallantly to win the war.

I hope our women in the United States will be worthy of the boys over here. I hope that we will be worthy of the women of Great Britain. Wistfully, a woman said to me when I happened to mention that I had seen one of my sons: "Mine is in the Near East and I haven't seen him for three years." Great Britain's sons are scattered far and wide, and so are ours. Let us resolve that we will do our part, giving whatever we have to give with the main object in view: the winning of the war as quickly as possible so that we may save as many lives as possible.

The women of Britain are helping to win the war. In fact, they are a very vital factor in the manpower of the nation. And they know, also, that they will be a very vital factor in making the peace and in carrying on the crusade which will certainly have to be carried on in the future.

Women may have had a feeling in the past that they did not have an equal responsibility with men in world affairs. The women of the future cannot have that feeling, because the writing on the wall is clear: That if there is to be peace in the world, women as well as men will have to decide to work and sacrifice to achieve it. The price of peace in the future may be sacrifices of material comforts in the years immediately after the war. Men, who have fought the war, and women, if they have given all they have to the war effort, may be tired when peace comes. But we cannot afford to be too tired to win the peace if our civilization is to go on. It cannot go on if wars continue, and I surmise that women will be a very potent factor in working out the necessary changes in existing economic systems, as well as changes in social conditions, which alone can bring real freedom to the people of the world.

The young people in high school and in college today—as well as those in the armed forces and industry and on the farms—will be a great factor in making these decisions of the future. If we decide to be selfish and to think of ourselves alone, for a time we may be able to achieve something which appears temporarily desirable. It seemed to be a desirable world we were creating in the United States in the 1920s. But the '30s were not very happy for many men, women, and young people. Like a Greek tragedy, the war moved forward in the wake of poverty. And disease and material and spiritual attrition inevitably fell upon nation after nation.

Our hope for the future, I believe, lies in the acceptance by women and young people of their responsibility. I think we failed before because we could not think on international lines. We did not have a broad enough vision. And the peoples of the world left their business in the hands of self-seekers, who thought of themselves and their temporary gains, but now and in the future you—the women and the youth of all the united nations—will have to awaken and accept full responsibility. It is no easy burden to assume. But if we win the battle over ourselves, the vision of God's world—ruled by justice and love—may become a reality.

# 35.

# "Wartime Conditions in Great Britain"

Wednesday, December 9, 1942, 10:15 p.m. (NBC Red Network)

ER: I have already talked a number of times on the radio about various phases of my trip to Great Britain, but I am glad of this opportunity to give a more detailed account of the situation there as I saw it.

Great Britain is a small island, so small that one of our boys inquiring as to how long it would take him by train to go from one point to another, when told what the distances were in every direction before he reached the sea, drew a long breath and said, "Gee, you tumble off quickly in any direction, don't you?" The whole area of Great Britain could be contained in any one of several of our states with ease. They are eighteen miles at some points from an enemy who has very good planes, is industrially well developed, and has one of the best trained and equipped armies in the world.

Three years ago, Great Britain was entirely unprepared to repel any real effort at invasion. Today, one gets the feeling that one is living in a fortress. Everywhere along the coast there is protection and the Home Guard is a very active body of people who are prepared to spring to arms in their own defense at any moment, quite aside from the regular army which is in Great Britain. Most of this army is in training but is available for defense at any point. There is now a network of sea and air defense such as was not dreamed of at the time of the Battle of Britain. But this little island has fronts all over the world where her men are fighting side by side with the men of the Dominions and, now, with the men from America.

The population of the whole island is some 46 million people, so it is perfectly obvious that they have had to use every bit of manpower that was available, and that includes the women and the young people of the nation. They have had to face many things which we, thank God, do not have to face. Up to the time of the beginning of the war, food for Great Britain came from every part of the world, and they only grew 47 percent of the food which they consumed. The Ministry of Agriculture has succeeded in raising that to nearly 60 percent, but they still have to obtain a great deal of their food supply from outside their own country, mainly from the United States, Canada, and South America. This means transportation, and transportation has to be taken up sometimes with getting an army to Africa and keeping it supplied with food and ammunition after it gets there.

In Great Britain, nothing must be made which is not necessary because labor and materials are precious. Great Britain is on a strict rationing system for food, for instance, because no one should have more than he needs to eat. It is probably true that a number of people in Great Britain whose diet was slim in the past may have a better-balanced diet than ever before. Every child under fourteen, Lord Woolton, the minister of food, told me, must have a pint of milk a day, and they pay for it when able. Otherwise, they get it free. Every young woman with a baby gets this same amount, but many other people in Great Britain use powdered milk, powdered eggs, and dehydrated food from the United States. And the roast beef of old England, for which she was justly famous, has practically disappeared from the table. One fresh egg a month is the civilian ration, as I discovered when we were breakfasting in one of our American Navy stations, and I happened to have beside me a young girl who was a private in the Army Auxiliary Service. I heard a little gasp as a plate was put down before her, and, on asking her what was the matter, she replied, "Oh, two months' rations all at once." I looked down to see that two fried eggs had been placed before her, from American Army rations, of course.

The people of Great Britain have learned to eat what they can get and to bear it without much complaining. They have learned to get only the clothes which their coupons allow them to have, and these cover only the necessities of life. You are lucky if you had enough left from prewar days to give you a few extra things to wear. If you are bombed out, some of the secondhand clothing, which the people of America have sent over, will be given to you at a distribution agency without your having to produce coupons to obtain them.

You will be telling me soon that none of this seems to have much relation to anything happening over here, and that you do not quite understand why it is of interest to you. My answer is that I think we have something to learn from the fact that people have lived on this island and developed protective devices which make life possible, and can still smile and look hopefully toward the future. They do discuss food. It does make a tremendous difference. For instance, if you bring some friend a gift from this country, say a box of hard candy or of chocolates, they thank you as they might have thanked you in the past for a diamond bracelet. Some bobby pins or a cake of soap are a gift from heaven.

You may laugh, but my short time spent over there has sharpened my appreciation of many of the things I used to take for granted over here. I walk down the street on a bright, sunny day and find myself re-peating, "What a wonderfully blue sky and how marvelous the sun is."

I will order a meal in a restaurant and remember that, over there, I had to choose carefully because I could not have both eggs and meat or fish at the same meal. I could have one and only one.

We haven't had to undergo bombing and I pray that we will never have to. Nevertheless, I have a very great admiration for the people of Great Britain, who have developed such steadfastness and calm during the concentrated blitzes that now they pay no attention to a sporadic raid here and there. In Dover, where shelling and enemy air sorties are frequent, we were being shown about the grounds near the houses which the Wrens occupy. The Wrens correspond to our Waves and do many things in the Navy to release men for other service.

The day we were there, the director's office in one of the buildings was having a new roof put on and they casually pointed to a hole in the ground and said, "That is where the bomb dropped yesterday." And then they showed me a tree between two buildings which had been badly scarred by the passing of a shell which had gone beyond through the shelter filled with girls. "We were very fortunate," my guide said, "only one girl's head was grazed by the shell."

The children in the streets, of course, can tell you whether the drone of a motor overhead is an enemy machine or one of their own. And they can tell you whether a bomb dropping is an incendiary bomb or something more harmful. Yet nobody seemed excited or even disturbed. Some people go into the shelters built into the cliffs if they think it is going to be a bad night, primarily because they want to be able to sleep and be ready for work in the morning, but not because they are afraid.

Somehow one feels these people are beyond fear, and they know the business of life must go on. They are able to bear whatever is their lot. I have come back with a tremendously increased confidence and admiration for the ability of human beings to stand up under difficulty and danger. I am sure we could do just what the British have done, but I hope we may not have to. I trust that we will be able to understand enough about the world in which we live so that we will truly allow all of our energies and all of our power to go into the organization of a world in which such things as this war cannot happen again.

Men and women in Great Britain—and children, too—are fighting this war day in and day out, hour in and hour out. They spend long hours in factories, give constant service in military establishments and civilian relief work, and through it all hope and confidence in the future never flags. They have time to strive to make the community in which they live a better community than ever before. And they consider such work a necessary part of the war effort. Many people have learned lessons which are lessons for all time, not just for the war period.

In Bristol, the Women's Voluntary Service, manned largely by housewives, use their mobile canteens—which fed the whole population during the blitz—in the more peaceful times they now enjoy to take midday and midnight meals to the dockworkers so they will not have to waste time leaving their work in search of food. One of the housewives told me that she had lived all her life in Bristol and had been rather fearful of the dockworkers; they were rough men, men who used bad language, who got drunk and were generally not the nice people of the town. But now they were her friends. They were keeping the lifeline open by loading and unloading ships as quickly as their strength would allow. And she would never feel again that gulf between herself and her neighbors.

Our boys who are in camps over there are learning a great deal too. They are learning what the homes in Great Britain are like, what the people are like, and that there is gratitude there for the generosity of people in this country in their hour of trial. Our boys have had to stand up under the same difficult climate as the British and I doubt if they like it in the autumn and winter. But at least they have American food in camp and are not restricted as the British are. They have their own canteens and it is lucky that they have, for the young American has a sweet tooth and can consume more candy and more sugar than one would think possible if one had not observed it. Even the paratroops have, as part of their rations, a cake of chocolate. And some of the boys tell me that on long marches hard candy is a tremendous help.

Our boys have a justifiable pride, I think, in their equipment. Their uniforms are good and they are well supplied. If we in private life find it hard here and there to get just what we want, it will give us satisfaction to know that the reason may be that our boys are getting more of the necessary clothes for whatever climate they may be in than is the case in any other army in the world.

They do have to learn a lot from experience. Most of them haven't liked woolen socks a great deal in the past, unless they were working in the woods or going on a skiing party or a long hike. Now they find that, at least in Great Britain, everyone wears woolen socks and they are pretty comfortable. If they scorned them at first when they were offered them, they hope they will have another chance to accept them.

They are getting good medical care, in many cases probably better than they would have at home. War is a job which hardens men both physically and mentally, and there are hazards which no amount of good equipment or preparation can prevent. But some of the boys who come through safely will perhaps have had certain chances to remedy physical defects which they might never have had in civilian life.

I said the other day that I wished we trained young officers, especially, for leading discussion groups. And one of the New York papers found an ex-sergeant of Marines who boiled over on the subject of what this would do in the way of softening the men. He just did not seem to realize that that was part of the mental toughening which many of the men need, and not my idea at all, but one that some of the best fighting men I have ever known have actually put into practice.

Out of this war will come men toughened physically and mentally, and knowing what they want in the future. But unless they also know how to go about getting it and how to really analyze the world situation, they will not be much use to us as citizens. No matter how good a soldier you are, your fundamental value is as a citizen in the future. Your boys, scattered over the world, are learning to be the best United States citizens possible, because they are learning about the world as a whole, of which the United States is just a part. We who stay at home must stretch our own horizons in every way possible, so when the boys return they will find us able to keep step with them mentally.

This is recognized in Great Britain, and many people are preparing for the postwar period now. The Beveridge Report [on British social security] shows how far their thinking has gone, and I think that we should be grateful that there are groups of people in and out of the government who are also planning for the future over here. No matter how well we plan, there must be a long period of readjustment, and the better we plan, the better we will be prepared to make that period count for the good of the whole world.

There are certain community services in Great Britain which I felt were not, as yet, sufficiently developed, and many people in Great Britain feel the same way. For instance, they have the same problem that we have about the schoolchild too old for a day nursery or nursery school, who attends school and yet is left for several hours—more hours in Great Britain than in this country, as yet—with mothers who work and no one to supervise the home. They are talking of what can be done to develop better supervision for these children so that the period between the actual closing of school and the time when workers return to their homes may not be a period of danger for the children and the young people.

I did not feel that in this field they had anything to offer us, as yet, and I hope that we will go on with the development of school use for after-school activities, and perhaps we may be able to originate some ideas which may be of use to them. They have the same problem with their girls of fourteen and fifteen that has cropped up in some places in the United States, where young boys are working in factories, as they now are also in England before they enter the military forces. There, as here, they make more money than they could have made in the past, more money than a soldier makes, with the result that unless wholesome and attractive leisure-time activities are developed for this fourteen-to-eighteen-year-old group, they will take to the entertainment provided for older people and will suffer in consequence.

It seemed to me also that, in connection with British restaurants, which are undoubtedly a godsend to all people with families who have to get food occasionally out of their own homes, in moderate-priced places there might be developed a service where people could order food and take it home with them. Of course, the evening meal is a fairly simple meal to get in Great Britain, so that the canteens in every factory, with their midday and midnight hot meals, and the universal school lunches for children in school, do mean a great relief and reduction in home cooking. We probably do more preparation for our evening meal than they do and it might be more important to us to have a home service than it is to them. This, of course, is only necessary in places where great numbers of women go from the homes to work on a full, daily schedule.

Over here we will probably never have the long hours which they have been forced to have in Great Britain. There is also a possibility of organizing neighborhoods into cooperative groups for filling these home needs. They acknowledge in Great Britain that it is better to work shorter hours, particularly for the women, but necessity and shortage of manpower drives them to the longer hours.

I have an idea that in this country we may feel our shortage of manpower more acutely on the farms than anywhere else. Perhaps the organization of a Land Army may be the most helpful pattern for us to study in Great Britain. The most outstanding thing about it to me was that training was given the women who entered the Land Army, that they were issued equipment and uniforms just as the auxiliary military services were. And that they had the same social-security benefits in health-insurance allowances and unemployment compensation that the factory workers had. They try, in England, to so organize their farms that they have at least a nucleus of workers who are all-the-year-round workers. Their farms are smaller and more diversified, and it is an easier problem than it is with us on some of our big ranches, which have primarily seasonal needs for a great number of workers. This problem, however, will have to be met in a special way, I imagine, with volunteers during the war period.

The regular supply of farm labor might be greatly helped over here by the organization of a Women's Land Army. The placement would, of course, be done through the regular employment service channels. The recruiting and training would probably be better done under the Department of Agriculture. Here, I think, we might find much help in a careful study of what the triumphs and disasters may have been in the development of the work in Great Britain. Ours would have to be a voluntary enlistment. Over there, these workers are drawn from the regular draft group. There is compulsory billeting over there so that if the farmer has not room to house and feed the workers, they can be put in houses in a nearby village and their board paid. Or the government sets up a hostel, probably in some unused country house where their board money is used in the general upkeep. Lady [Trudie] Denman, who heads this group in England, might be one of the people it would be helpful for us to consult over here.

Some of our American girls who are in the Ferry Command in Great Britain, flying all kinds of airships from place to place within the island, must be getting an opportunity to see something of the work of a great many of the British girls. I wonder if, from time to time, it might not be a good idea to ask some of them to report to us their impressions over the radio from Great Britain. Fresh points of view that come to us from people who are actually doing work in faraway countries, it seems to me, would be helpful in understanding the world situation as it develops. I hope that our War Information service may occasionally be able to arrange this for us.

In closing, I think I will tell you the two things which seem to be the most important to the boys from the US that I saw in Great Britain, many of whom are now in Africa. One was mail, the other was pay. I am sure that in their letters you have had these same things come up. Why don't they get their pay on time? Why don't they get their letters? The answer is that when men move about, and they do move from camp to camp within Great Britain, and suddenly from this country to other parts of the world, and from their first destinations to new destinations, it is sometimes very difficult to work out the mere mechanics of getting their paychecks on the date due and of having the mail reach its destination as quickly as possible. I think every effort should be made by the departments involved to improve both of these things as rapidly as possible. But where the pay is concerned, I think the most important thing is that allotments to families should be promptly paid. After all, the men are taken care of as far as their actual needs are concerned, but family needs cannot wait. Even then, I do not think that we should ever be complacent over any shortcomings, and I hope that both these things will eventually be improved.

# 36.

# "D-Day Message"

## June 6, 1944 (NBC Blue Network)

On June 6, 1944, a massive force of Allied fighters landed on a fifty-mile ribbon of Nazi-occupied French coastline in Normandy. The attack by 160,000 Allied troops was the largest amphibious invasion in history and a turning point in the war against Germany. FDR had addressed the nation in a Fireside Chat the evening before, marking the fall of Rome to Allied forces. As he spoke, Allied ships were crossing the English Channel. Early on the morning of June 6, radio listeners heard the first bulletins from London that the D-Day invasion had begun. CBS and NBC broadcast in-depth war news throughout the day. At ten p.m., President Roosevelt went on the air to read a prayer for the troops storming the French coastline. Earlier in the day, ER went on NBC to rally the women of America who had loved ones taking part in the fight.

ER: It is a great privilege to have this opportunity to speak to the women of this country at this time, when they are undergoing such a great strain. I am speaking particularly, of course, to those who have men they love—husbands, sons, brothers, sweethearts, or very dear friends—taking an active part in the European invasion or stationed anywhere in the areas where there may be intensified activity during the next few weeks.

We know that, in the end, we will win. But we do not know what the cost will be. The only thing I can say to you is that every woman, no matter what her church affiliation may be, will be praying daily that the victory will be speedy, and that this time the sacrifices, whatever they are, will bring results which will justify in the eyes of those who fight whatever they may have gone through.

All that science can do to protect our men will be done, and to the care of the wounded will be added all that human devotion can do. We may be sure that all that can be done to alleviate suffering and save human lives, will be done.

All that we at home can do, however, is to pray, and to prepare ourselves to fulfill our obligations to those who fight. They will feel we have backed them up in attaining their objectives if we use our citizenship to attain the ends for which they sacrifice. It is not enough to win the fight; we must win that for which we fight. In this case, it is the triumph of all people who believe that the people of the world are worthy of freedom and that no race has a right to seek domination over any other, so that we ultimately build a permanent peace.

May we have the courage to do our part for the sake of future generations. And may God bring consolation to those who suffer both at home and abroad.

# 37.

# "V-E Day Radio Message"

## May 8, 1945, 11:25 a.m. (NBC Red Network)

President Franklin D. Roosevelt died of a cerebral hemorrhage on April 12, 1945, at his cottage in Warm Springs, Georgia. Vice President Harry S. Truman was sworn in as commander-in-chief. The Allies were on the verge of victory in Europe; Hitler committed suicide in his Berlin bunker eighteen days later. His successor signed a document of unconditional surrender on May 7 in a French schoolhouse. Victory in Europe Day, or V-E Day, was celebrated in the United States on May 8, 1942. Eleanor Roosevelt spoke to the nation from the NBC studios in New York. ER urged her listeners to stay resolute. There was still a war to win against Japan in the Pacific.

ER: I am very happy to have this opportunity to speak to the people of this country on V-E Day. It is a day on which we can be happy that the European war is at an end.

I know my husband would want me to say to you, the soldiers of this country on all the fields of battle, and to the workers at home and the civilians who, side by side, have won through to this day with him, that he is grateful to each and every one of you. I think, also, that he would want to say that we must go on with every power we have until the war is fully won. And that after that, we must give all the backing we can to our own president, to the heads of allied nations, and win through to a permanent peace. That was the main objective for which my husband fought. That is the goal which we must never lose sight of.

It will be difficult. And there will be times when it will be hard to understand other nations and their leaders. But the goal is there. And in one way or another, our leaders and our people must fight through to a permanent peace. That is the only way that we, as a nation, can feel compensation for the sacrifice of thousands of young lives in our own country and in other countries.

Today, I think I want to say again, thank you, from my husband and from myself, as a private citizen. Because it is a wonderful thing to be a private citizen, standing side by side with all other citizens of this great country, knowing that our leaders are worthy and that, we, as citizens, will be worthy of them.

# 38.

# "V-J Day Radio Message"

## Tuesday, August 14, 1945 (CBS)

On August 15, 1945, Emperor Hirohito of Japan went on the radio to tell his people that Japan was giving up. Because of the difference in time zones, it was a day earlier in the United States. After President Harry S. Truman announced the Japanese surrender at a press conference, Americans swarmed to town and city centers across the country, creating spontaneous parades and rallies. Others marked the victory with prayer services at houses of worship.

The victory came after Truman's decision to drop atomic bombs on the Japanese cities of Hiroshima and Nagasaki. This new and powerful military technology was vaguely understood by the American public. In her broadcast to the nation on V-J Day, Eleanor Roosevelt rightly predicted that the new weapon would challenge the wisdom of humanity. She proposed that atomic science should be collectively developed and controlled.

ER called on the women of the world to help create a constructive and lasting peace. She would play her own influential role in shaping the postwar world. President Truman appointed her a delegate to the newly created United Nations on March 15, 1946. Until her death in 1962, ER would travel the globe promoting peace and international cooperation.

ER: The day for which the people of the world have prayed is here at last. There is great thankfulness in our hearts. Peace has not come, however, as the result of the kind of power which we have known in the past, but as the result of a new discovery which, as yet, is not fully understood, nor even developed.

There is a certain awe and fear coupled with our rejoicing today. Because we know that there are new forces in the world, partly understood but not, as yet, completely developed and controlled. This new force is a tremendous challenge to the wisdom of men. For that reason, I know that most of us feel that it must be subject to their collective wisdom. Just as it was discovered by the pooling of knowledge from men of many races and religions, so it must be ruled in its development. We should not think only of its destructive power, for this new discovery may hold within it the germs of the greatest good that man has ever known. But that good can only be achieved through man's wisdom in developing and controlling it.

Today we have a mixture of emotions. Joy that our men are freed of constant danger. Hope that those whom we love will soon be home among us. Awe at what man's intelligence can encompass. And a realization that that intelligence, uncontrolled by great spiritual forces, can be man's destruction instead of his salvation.

For the happy wives and mothers of my own country and of the world, my heart rejoices today. But I cannot forget that to many, this moment only adds a poignancy to their grief. All women—wives and mothers, sisters or sweethearts—who have had men involved in this conflict know what it is to live with fear as a constant companion. Some women will still have to help their men fight the aftermath of war in their own lives. Others have lost forever the men they held dear. Many, many women, however, will be able to rejoice for themselves individually, and for the others whose anxiety for their dear ones and whose separation from them will soon be over.

Many of us are hoping that the very suffering which women of all nationalities have been through will bring about a greater kinship among them than has ever existed before. The power of women for good should be intensified, because they will surely determine to work together in order to ensure that the forces of the world are used for constructive purposes.

Women want to create a world atmosphere in which human beings may develop in peace and loving understanding. Our prayer today is one of gratitude, O Lord, that peace has come to bless the Earth. But above all, we pray for wisdom and for the spirit of love in the hearts of men, for without that spirit, wisdom will avail us little.

Before closing, I want to say just one word about my husband. I know that many people have thought of him very constantly, ever since the war came to an end. I am deeply grateful. He always felt that we could and would fight this war to ultimate victory. And he had complete assurance that the victory, once won, the people of the United States would turn their full strength and power into making peace a reality and a benefit to mankind.

# Notes

## Introduction

1. Eleanor Roosevelt, *This I Remember* (New York: Harper Brothers, 1949), 232.

2. Radio script, "The Pan-American Coffee Bureau," December 7, 1941, Papers of Eleanor Roosevelt, Franklin D. Roosevelt Library, Hyde Park NY (hereafter ER Papers), box 1411.

3. ER quoted in Blanche Wiesen Cook, *Eleanor Roosevelt, Volume One 1884–1933* (New York: Penguin Books, 1992), 425.

4. Blanche Wiesen Cook, *Eleanor Roosevelt, Volume Two 1933–1938* (New York: Penguin Books, 1999), 67.

5. Lawrence W. Levine and Cornelia R. Levine, *The People and the President: America's Conversation with FDR* (Boston: Beacon Press, 2002), 23–24.

6. "Eleanor Everywhere," *Time*, November 20, 1933.

7. Rita S. Halle, "That First Lady of Ours," *Good Housekeeping*, December 1933.

8. Cook, *Volume Two*, 3.

9. Maurine H. Beasley, *Eleanor Roosevelt and the Media: A Public Quest for Self-Fulfillment* (Chicago: University of Illinois Press, 1987), 3.

10. Cook, *Volume Two*, 339.

11. Quoted in *Heinl Radio Business Letter*, May 29, 1934. Library of American Broadcasting, University of Maryland, College Park, MD.

12. Maurine Beasley, *Eleanor Roosevelt: Transformative First Lady* (Lawrence: University Press of Kansas, 2010), 85.

13. Virginia Pasley, "First Lady to the Common Man," *American Mercury*, March 1944.

14. Blanche Wiesen Cook, in preface to *What I Hope to Leave Behind: The Essential Essays of Eleanor Roosevelt*, ed. Alida Black (Brooklyn, New York: Carlson Publishing, 1995), xiii.

15. Letter to ER, January 19, 1933. ER Papers, box 12.

16. Letter to ER, April 30, 1940. ER Papers, Radio Listener Mail (small collections), box 4.

17. Letter to ER, February 24, 1942. ER Papers, Radio Listener Mail (small collections), box 6.

18. Quoted in *Dear Mrs. Roosevelt: Letters from Children of the Great Depression*, ed. Robert Cohen (Chapel Hill: University of North Carolina Press, 2002), 182.

19. Postcard to ER, January 23, 1933, ER Papers, box 12.

20. Letter to ER, January 12, 1933, ER Papers, box 12.

21. Letters to ER, January 14 and January 31, 1933, ER Papers, box 12.

22. "Liberal Mrs. Roosevelt," *Radio Guide*, December 11, 1932.

23. "A Matter of Propriety," *The Hartford Courant*, December 20, 1932.

24. John T. Flynn, *Country Squire in the White House* (New York: Doubleday, Doran and Company, 1940), 107–12.

25. Westbrook Pegler syndicated column in the *Ogden* [Utah] *Standard Examiner*, August 13, 1945.

26. Cook, *Volume Two*, 484.

27. J.E. Doyle, "Hearst Radio Editors' Annual Poll," *Radio Stars*, April 1938.

28. Eleanor Roosevelt, *This I Remember*, 73.

29. Jason Loviglio, *Radio's Intimate Public: Network Broadcasting and Mass-Mediated Democracy* (Minneapolis: University of Minnesota Press, 2005), xix.

30. Anne McCormick, "Radio: A Great Unknown Force," *The New York Times*, March 27, 1932.

31. Anne McCormick, "Radio's Audience: Huge, Unprecedented," *The New York Times*, April 3, 1932.

32. Susan Douglas, *Listening In: Radio and the American Imagination* (Minneapolis: University of Minnesota Press, 1999), 20.

33. John B. Kennedy, "Ladies of the Air Waves," *Collier's*, July 9, 1932.

34. Hadley Cantril and Gordon W. Allport, *The Psychology of Radio* (Salem, NH: Ayer Publishing Company, 1935), 208.

35. John K. Hutchens, "The Secret of a Good Radio Voice," *The New York Times*, December 6, 1942.

36. "Mrs. Franklin D. Roosevelt," *Variety*, December 13, 1932.

37. R. Calvert Haws, "Air Secrets of the President's Wife," *Radio Guide*, November 16, 1935.

38. James F. Bender, "Their Voices Soft and Low," *The New York Times*, September 9, 1945.

39. Samuel I. Rosenman, *Working with Roosevelt* (New York: Da Capo Press, 1972), 11.

40. Lawrence W. Levine and Cornelia Levine, *The Fireside Conversations: America Responds to FDR During the Great Depression* (Berkeley: University of California Press, 2010), 13.

41. Roosevelt, *This I Remember*, 162.

42. "Six Figures," *The New Yorker*, February 29, 1936.

43. Arthur Krock, "My Day Anticipates and Echoes Press Conferences," *The New York Times*, August 10, 1939.

44. Cook, *Volume Two*, 37.

45. Rosenman, *Working with Roosevelt*, 346.

46. Doris Kearnes Goodwin, *No Ordinary Time—Franklin and Eleanor Roosevelt: The Home Front in World War II* (New York: Touchstone 1994), 629.

47. Allida M. Black, *Casting Her Own Shadow: Eleanor Roosevelt and the Shaping of Postwar Liberalism* (New York: Columbia University Press, 1996), 2.

48. Letter to ER, July 28, 1940. ER Papers, Radio Listener Mail (small collections), box 1.

49. Letters to ER, September 13, 1934, ER papers, box 449.

## 1. "The Girl of Today"

1. Maurine H. Beasley, Holly C. Shulman, and Henry R. Beasley, eds., *The Eleanor Roosevelt Encyclopedia* (Westport, CT: Greenwood Press, 2001), 423.

2. Joseph P. Lash, *Eleanor and Franklin: The Story of their Relationship Based on Eleanor Roosevelt's Private Papers*, (New York: Norton 1971), 356.

3. Letter to ER, December 20, 1932. ER Papers, box 12.

4. Undated letter to ER. ER Papers, box 12.

5. Letter to ER, December 14, 1932. ER Papers, box 12.

6. Telegram to ER, December 17, 1932. ER Papers, box 12.

7. ER to W.E. Graves, January 25, 1934. ER Papers, box 12.

8. Susan Ware, *Holding Their Own: American Women in the 1930s* (New York: Twayne Publishers, 1982), 27.

9. Eleanor Roosevelt, *This I Remember* (New York: Harper and Brothers, 1949), 13.

10. Eleanor Roosevelt, "The Girl of Today," radio script, December 9, 1932, ER Papers, box 1397.

**5. "Negro Education"**

1. Allida M. Black, *Casting Her Own Shadow: Eleanor Roosevelt and the Shaping of Postwaar Liberalism* (New York: Columbia University Press, 1996), 37.

2. Blanche Wiesen Cook, *Eleanor Roosevelt, Volume Two 1933–1938* (New York: Penguin Books, 1999), 185.

**6. "When Will a Woman Become President of the US?"**

1. Dick Templeton, "Summer Radio—First Lady On Air for $3,000," *The Microphone*, May 19, 1934.

**9. "Peace Through Education"**

1. Allida M. Black, *Casting Her Own Shadow: Eleanor Roosevelt and the Shaping of Postwar Liberalism* (New York: Columbia University Press, 1996), 138.

2. Letter to ER, December 25, 1934. ER Papers, box 449.

**10. "World Court Broadcast"**

1. "Coughlin Renews World Court Fight," *The New York Times*, January 28, 1935.

2. "First Lady Urges World Court Step," *The New York Times*, January 28, 1935.

**11. "Making the Wheels Go 'Round in the White House"**

1. R. Calvert Hawes and Edyth Dixon, "Air Secrets of the President's Wife," *Radio Guide*, November 16, 1935.

**17. "Eleanor Roosevelt Interviewed on the Causes and Cures of War"**

1. Alida M. Black, *Casting Her Own Shadow: Eleanor Roosevelt and the Shaping of Postwar Liberalism* (New York: Columbia University Press, 1996), 137.

**18. "Domestic Workers and Government Housing"**

1. Lynne Olson, *Those Angry Days: Roosevelt, Lindbergh, and America's Fight over World War II* (New York: Random House, 2013), 33.

2. "First Lady's Week," *Time*, April 15, 1940.

3. Dorothy Dunbar Bromley, "The Future of Eleanor Roosevelt," *Harper's*, January 1940.

4. Letter to ER, June 20, 1940. ER Papers, ER Radio Listener Mail, box 5.

5. Letter to ER, July 24, 1940. ER Papers, ER Radio Listener Mail, box 5.

## 24. "Address to the Democratic National Convention"

1. Jean Edward Smith, *FDR* (New York: Random House, 2007), 459.

2. Eleanor Roosevelt, *This I Remember* (New York: Harper and Brothers, 1949), 214.

## 25. "Shall We Arm Merchant Ships?"

1. "Text of Lindbergh Address in Indiana," *The Milwaukee Sentinel*, October 5, 1941.

2. Maurine Beasley, *Eleanor Roosevelt: Transformative First Lady* (Lawrence: University Press of Kansas, 2010), 182.

3. ER quoted in Allida M. Black, *Casting Her Own Shadow: Eleanor Roosevelt and the Shaping of Postwar Liberalism* (New York: Columbia University Press, 1996), 143.

4. Beasley, *Transformative First Lady*, 193.

## 29. "Pearl Harbor Attack"

1. "Radio First to Nation with News of Jap Attack," *PM*, December 8, 1941.

2. James Cannon, "Corporal Jimmy Cannon Says," *PM*, December 8, 1941.

## 34. "Broadcast from Liverpool"

1. James P. Lash, *Eleanor and Franklin: The Story of Their Relationship Based on Eleanor Roosevelt's Private Papers* (New York: Norton, 1971), 657.

2. "Mrs. Roosevelt's Postscript," *The Times*, London, England, November 9, 1942.

3. Lash, *Eleanor and Franklin*, 668.

# About the Author

Stephen Drury Smith is the executive editor and host of American RadioWorks® (ARW), the acclaimed national documentary series from American Public Media®. Smith and ARW have been awarded the DuPont-Columbia University Gold and Silver Batons. He has covered a wide range of international and domestic issues, including human rights, science and health, education, race relations, and American history. He is a co-editor (with Catherine Ellis) of *Say It Plain: A Century of Great African American Speeches* and *Say It Loud: Great Speeches on Civil Rights and African American Identity* and (with Mary Marshall Clark, Peter Bearman, and Catherine Ellis) of *After the Fall: New Yorkers Remember September 2001 and the Years That Followed,* all published by The New Press. He lives in St. Paul, Minnesota, and Boston, Massachusetts.

# Publishing in the Public Interest

Thank you for reading this book published by The New Press. The New Press is a nonprofit, public interest publisher. New Press books and authors play a crucial role in sparking conversations about the key political and social issues of our day.

We hope you enjoyed this book and that you will stay in touch with The New Press. Here are a few ways to stay up to date with our books, events, and the issues we cover:

- Sign up at www.thenewpress.com/subscribe to receive updates on New Press authors and issues and to be notified about local events
- Like us on Facebook: www.facebook.com/newspressbooks
- Follow us on Twitter: www.twitter.com/thenewpress

Please consider buying New Press books for yourself; for friends and family; or to donate to schools, libraries, community centers, prison libraries, and other organizations involved with the issues our authors write about.

The New Press is a 501(c)(3) nonprofit organization. You can also support our work with a tax-deductible gift by visiting www.thenew press.com/donate.